Praise for TOP PERFORMER

"*I found John's material when I was recovering from a spinal cord injury and it literally changed my life forever. His books and his audio video material have been a guide to transitioning from NHL hockey player to a valuable member of the C- level business community.*"

> – Doug Smith
> President, Doug Smith Enterprises and
> second overall draft pick for the LA Kings

"*John Kanary has dedicated over 40 years to helping people from all walks of life work with their inner potential. He has been a mentor and friend to me and many others all over the world. John's sincere desire to help others succeed is gift-wrapped in the pages of this must-read book.*"

> – Perry Catena
> CFP IG Wealth Management

"*John Kanary is a visionary leader that has dedicated his life to coaching others. His understanding of the psychology of success has been the key to the strategies that he has shared for over 40 years!*"

> – Brian H Mennis
> Author of "Average To Awesome"

"*John Kanary provides a set of tools that are simple to understand and more importantly to implement and to improve the quality of every area of successful living.*"

> – Jane Kosti
> Executive Senior Director, Mary Kay

Published by
Hasmark Publishing
www.hasmarkpublishing.com

Disclaimer

This book is designed to provide information and motivation to our readers. It is sold with the understanding that the publisher is not engaged to render any type of psychological, legal, or any other kind of professional advice. The content of each article is the sole expression and opinion of its author, and not necessarily that of the publisher. No warranties or guarantees are expressed or implied by the publisher's choice to include any of the content in this volume. Neither the publisher nor the individual author(s) shall be liable for any physical, psychological, emotional, financial, or commercial damages, including, but not limited to, special, incidental, consequential or other damages. Our views and rights are the same: You are responsible for your own choices, actions, and results.

Permission should be addressed in writing to John Kanary at [mailing or email address]

Editor: Corinne Casazza
corinnecasazza@gmail.com

Book Design: Anne Karklins
annekarklins@gmail.com

ISBN 13: 978-1-989161-63-0
ISBN 10: 1989161634

TOP
PERFORMER

HOW TO GET THERE
AND HOW TO STAY THERE

JOHN KANARY
FOREWORD BY BOB PROCTOR

Acknowledgements

Peggy McColl
You make it look so easy.

Perry Catena
Thanks for being there.

Jase Miles Perez
Could not have done this without you.

Brian Mennis
Appreciate all of your support.

Jon Jurus
Thanks buddy.

Bobby and Linda
You were there every step of the way.

TABLE OF CONTENTS

FOREWORD

My friendship with John Kanary goes back almost 50 years. If you mention the words "Top Performer," I think of none other than John Kanary.

Years ago, John attended every seminar I delivered, and I knew he understood the materials because he was the top salesman in the world for the company he worked for at that time. John not only understood the information, he lived it!

The very first book I wrote is called "You Were Born Rich" and there's a segment in one of my chapters where I talk about John Kanary. Rather than rewriting it to share with you, we have included the excerpt here for your benefit.

. . .

PERSISTENCE ALWAYS PAYS

A number of years ago, John Kanary, a friend and former business partner of mine, was discussing Hill's chapter on "persistence" with me. We both seemed to be equally impressed with the importance of this quality, as well as with the necessity of a person having it, if they were to reach any worthwhile goal.

After a time and nearing the end of our discussion, we each agreed we would read the chapter on "persistence," once every day for thirty days. I don't even have to ask John to find out if this exercise helped him – I know it did; and the exercise has most certainly benefited me on numerous occasions.

There's an interesting story concerning John Kanary, which would be very appropriate to share with you here, since it illustrates both the power of "imaging," as well as "persistence."

Although I had known John Kanary for a couple of years and had talked with him on many occasions, I certainly did not know him as intimately as I do at the time of this writing. It is important that I bring this out here, as I will be referring back to it shortly. The incident I am about to relate, took place in 1971.

I was living in Chicago at the time and had just completed a speaking engagement in Edmonton, Alberta. When I returned to my room, there was a telephone message for me to call John Kanary, in Belleville, Ontario, Canada. I returned the call and after a couple of minutes of small talk, John said it was rather important that he meet with me, as he had something he wanted to discuss and he preferred not to "go into it" on the telephone. I asked John to wait while I looked over my calendar; it was, in the vernacular – packed tight. I was busy, to say the least; almost every day I had either a seminar or speaking engagement in a different city in North America. I explained this to John and told him that although I would love to visit, I really didn't know when I could. John was persistent, so I said, "Listen, I'm leaving Edmonton for Chicago tonight at midnight. To get to Chicago I have to go through Toronto. I'll arrive there at 7 a.m. I'll have to change terminals and I leave from the second terminal, one hour and fifty minutes later. I'll be happy to talk to you then, although I don't promise to be too alert after flying all night."

It's also worth mentioning that John had to get up early enough to drive the 125 miles from Belleville to Toronto, to meet my 7:00 a.m. arrival. I remember all John said was, "I'll be there."

The next morning I sat in the airport coffee shop and listened as John explained how he wanted to do what I was doing. He wanted to conduct seminars. He also explained that he was prepared to pay the price, whatever it might be.

As I listened, it was like hearing a popular song on the radio – you keep hearing it, over and over again. In almost every seminar I conduct there's a man or woman in the seminar who wants to do what I am doing. I've heard it in Biloxi, Mississippi; Butte, Montana; Los Angeles, New York, Moncton and Montreal – it was an old tune. Now, here I was in Toronto with a friend who, as I have already mentioned, I didn't know that well, and he was asking what he had to do.

As I was listening, the same images, which I had with all the others, were flashing through my mind. I was remembering all the travelling and the fear of standing up and speaking in a large hotel ballroom crowded with people who wanted you to get them excited, but who were mentally putting you on trial at the same time, thinking, "Does this guy know what he's talking about?" In many situations, such as a sales convention, you had forty minutes from beginning to end in which to build rapport with a few hundred strangers and get them excited about themselves.

The years of staying up nights reading and studying, the years of learning by attending seminars all over the continent, the years of working for next to nothing to prepare oneself to hold the attention of a group of people all day in a seminar, these were the images racing across my mind. It had taken me eleven years to get to that point.

But how do you say, "No, you'll never do it," when someone like John asks you, especially when the essence of what you teach is – you can do anything. Yet, how can you say "yes," when everyone you know, with the exception of two or three others besides yourself, can't earn a living in the public speaking business unless they're a celebrity. (And that is a whole different story.)

When John Kanary finished, I told him what I had told all the others: "Yes, you can do it, but it's tough. Make sure you understand that, John. It's tough. You'll have to do a tremendous amount of studying, because you not only have to know what to say, but you must also have the answers to a thousand and one questions arising as a result of what you say. Some of the questions will come from professional people – medical doctors, engineers and lawyers – who, in most cases, know what they're talking about. So, you not only have to be right, but confident as well, or you'll be discredited with your entire audience; and that only has to happen a couple of times and you're "out of business."

You not only have to study these ideas, but you must use them as well, or there'll be no conviction in your talks. (Not to mention the fact that you'll be a walking physical contradiction to what you teach.) It's next to impossible, for example, to have a sick person teaching 'health.'

You must develop showmanship and voice control, and on and on it goes. In short, John, for every one who makes it, a thousand fail miserably."

Usually when this is explained, the person says they still want to go ahead, but you never hear from them again. John was no exception, in one sense – he still wanted to go ahead. However, in every other way he was an exception. I did see him again. I told him what to read and what to do and he read it and did it. John read hundreds of books – he "devoured" them. He narrated them onto tapes and then played the tapes in the car. At his own expense, he followed me all over the country and sat in hundreds of seminars. He wrote thousands of pages of notes and studied them diligently.

Finally, I would have him open and close the seminars. Then he would conduct part of a seminar himself. In the beginning he was full of fear, he was soaking wet. Sometimes he'd be so worried about what the audience thought of him, that he would forget everything he knew and, as you know, an audience can be very cruel. But despite all this he continued. (Keep in mind this was costing him money; he was not being paid.)

John Kanary had built an image of himself doing "what I was doing" and he would not quit. He was persistent and it worked. It always has and it always will. Today he has earned the respect of many of the world's largest corporations. He has spoken in almost every major city in North America. He has also earned more in one day than he was earning in a year when I first met him!

So, if someone with numerous degrees after their name tells you Image-Making and Persistence don't work, just look up John Kanary and ask him. He'll tell you, "I know you can do it, because I did it!"

~ Bob Proctor

INTRODUCTION

"God's gift to us is more talent than we can use in one lifetime. Our gift to God is to develop as much of this talent as we can, in this lifetime."

– Steve Bow

"The highest reward for a person's toil is not what they get for it, but what they become by it."

– John Ruskin

• • •

Welcome, friend,

Thank you for purchasing *Top Performer*. In this book you'll find a user-friendly, step-by-step guide to happiness, achievement and creating the life of your dreams.

My name is John Kanary. For the past 40 years, I've provided prosperity and leadership coaching to some of the most successful companies and individuals in the world. I've worked with new and established companies, tech giants and sports franchises, private clients and crowds of thousands.

I've witnessed with my own eyes a stunning variety of human achievement, and I'm grateful that my work has allowed me to be an eternal student of the universal laws of attraction, compensation and return.

Most of all, I have learned over and over – as you will! – that success and fulfillment are not magic, given to a lucky few from on-high for reasons beyond our reach. No no no!

Success can be learned. Fulfillment can learned.

Anyone can reach them. Anyone can have them. You can reach them. You can have them.

If you know what you want and you're willing to put in the work, know that whatever you desire is yours for the taking.

You can start becoming a Top Performer as soon as you like.

How about today?

How about now?

. . .

I have good news.

Each and every concept in this book is extremely, beautifully simple.

Almost nothing you'll encounter in *Top Performer* has been *simplified*, manipulated or stripped of substance for the average reader to understand. This isn't one of those books.

The exercises contained in these pages can be completed with a pen and paper (and of course, *action!*). In my experience, there's no place more filled with fear, wonder and possibility than a blank page. You can change just about anything if you're willing to find the right words.

So, if what follows seems straightforward and clear that's because... well…it is.

But let's be equally clear about this – *simple* doesn't mean *easy*.

Changing your life is hard. Becoming a Top Performer is hard. Living *your* best life – the one *only you* could dream of and *only you* can create and sustain – is an art. Your life should be your masterpiece and mastery isn't easy.

But it is *simple*.

I've structured *Top Performer* as a progression of ten lessons, each focusing on a different principle of personal development, prosperity and success. When **practiced** together with dedication and passion, these principles *will* manifest results of remarkable abundance and joy in your life.

Anyone can do this. I've seen it work for myself and my clients countless times. Do the work. Don't skip steps, don't settle for anything less than your best effort. This process works.

In the coming Chapters, here is what you can expect –

. . .

CHAPTER 1

What are the characteristics of a Top Performer? What is the Achievement Pyramid? How do I prepare for the journey I am about to take?

CHAPTER 2

What's the first step to becoming a Top Performer? How do I begin to set a course toward a worthy vision? How do I align myself with positive, powerful attitudes and expectations?

CHAPTER 3-5

What is the difference between purpose, visions and Goals? Why is each necessary and valuable? What are **my** Goals, Visions and Purpose?

CHAPTER 6-7

How can I put the Top Performer qualities to work in the world? How does being a Top Performer apply to selling and how do the principles of selling (Effective Communication & AIDARS) apply to life?

CHAPTER 8

What is a Mastermind Group? How do I establish connections, friendships and networks with other Top Performers? How do we inspire and hold each other accountable to new and ever-greater success?

CHAPTER 9

How have other people used these practices to achieve their dreams? How does being a Top Performer work in the world beyond these pages?

CHAPTER 10

What now? What next?

· · ·

By the end of this book you'll be well on your way to building and sustaining new habits of prosperity and fulfillment. You'll be authentically moving in the direction of your purpose. You'll be excited about your future. You'll be off and running.

There's a Buddhist proverb –

When the student is ready, the teacher appears.

Well, you purchased this book, didn't you?

You have dreams, don't you?

You've come this far.

You're ready.

CHAPTER 1
THE 10 CHARACTERISTICS OF TOP PERFORMERS AND THE ACHIEVEMENT PYRAMID

These lessons have been carefully crafted to make you reevaluate, progression by progression, what you're capable of doing and earning.

Top Performers are acutely aware that they must not only think, but *embody* the principles of success in order to thrive. This will involve the body, the conscious mind, and the subconscious mind.

I've had the pleasure of knowing many Top Performers over the years, and though their backgrounds and aspirations have varied widely, I have found they all have certain characteristics in common. They are –

· · ·

I. *The Top Performer understands there's no known method by which anyone can determine what you can accomplish in a given period of time. Your potential as a Top Performer is boundless.*

II *Top Performers are continually improving their results while decreasing their workload.*

III *Top Performers are continually accomplishing more in shorter periods of time.*

IV *Top Performers continually have a goal or objective they are pursuing.*

V *Top Performers must be able to see how they can reach their goals by improving their effectiveness in the necessary areas of their lives.*

VI *Top Performers are emotionally involved in the achievement of their goals, visions and purpose.*

VII *Top Performers continually operate on a creative plain, never on a competitive plain. They never allow standards or precedents to influence their objectives.*

VIII *Top Performers are acutely aware of the difference between work and leisure.*

IX *Top Performers always keep service and the wellbeing of others foremost in their minds.*

X *Top Performers are always involved in a planned program of personal happiness and self- development.*

...

This is how the *Top Performer* lives. It's more than something to do – it's a way to be.

Growing accustomed to this way of being is a dynamic, gradual process. It doesn't happen all at once. Yes, your thinking will likely change; however, much of that change will be a consequence of your actions (and therefore your results) changing dramatically.

And so, you must be prepared both for change and to change.

The shift in outward results is almost always the aftermath of inward movement. You can't have the prize unless you become the thing.

Another important point:

One does not need professional ambition to be a Top Performer!

The single parent who raises a beautiful family in difficult circumstances is a Top Performer.

The community organizer who develops and improves their neighborhood is a Top Performer.

The little league coach who teaches teamwork to generations of children is a Top Performer.

Top Performers are everywhere. You can use these concepts to achieve just about anything.

Transcending expectations, shattering barriers and boundaries, giving and giving and giving the best of yourself and loving your life is what being a Top Performer is about.

Set your sights on abundance and you can have it.

And if that bounty includes financial gain, you can have that too.

· · ·

You might be asking, *How do I start?*

We begin with imagination.

A powerful and active imagination is what keeps our spiritual house in order. It's as crucial as any other element in attracting all things requisite for the fulfillment of our desires. Think of imagination as, say, a cosmic chiropractor. When used properly, it aligns you with the the harmonious vibrations of the Law of Attraction. In other words, to become a Top Performer, you have to be able to imagine yourself as a Top Performer.

Beyond simply imagining, we need to organize and plan according to our imagination. The Top Performer creates life by harnessing and directing the power of imagination.

There are many ways to go about this. Personally, because I think in pictures, I like translating my goals into images.

Try this now.

(*Note: This technique works for me. Use it for yourself, modifying as you go, if needed until you find a practice that works best for you.*)

- Draw a pyramid
- At the very top, write the word purpose
- At one end of the base, write the word vision
- At the other end, write the word goals
- At the bottom, under the base, write the word strategy

Notice the word at the top. Purpose. The most important thing we can have in life is purpose. And although purpose can be kind of nebulous, it gives definition to everything else. It sets the precedent. Without purpose, actions are aimless.

(*For example, I've always believed my purpose in life is to create leaders and teach the principles of leadership. Nothing gives me greater satisfaction than empowering people to become better than they presently are, so they might lead and develop others the same way. That's my Purpose.*)

Visions and Goals are more precise.

Goals are the small, tactical steps – the strategies – we take to achieve our visions. Goals are short term, visions long term.

Once you have achieved or surpassed your goals and visions, set new goals and new visions. But your purpose, if articulated honestly, will rarely (if ever) change.

So for let's say, for instance, you've decided your purpose is to educate. In that case your first vision (how you *live* that purpose) might be to become a great school teacher. Naturally, this would involve many smaller steps – gaining your teaching license, getting a job, doing it well and so on.

Now you've become a great teacher; you've achieved that vision. But you're getting restless. Your purpose is still to educate, but you want to express it in a different way. Now you want to start your own school – build it and grow it from scratch. This will require a whole new set of strategic goals, with each bringing you step-by-step closer to achieving your vision as you live your purpose. If you're ever bored or uninspired, you're doing something wrong or you need to reevaluate your goals and visions. If you're feeling constantly challenged and inspired, you're on the right track.

Making sense so far?

So, to summarize:

We use goals to *strategically* achieve our visions while always, always living our *purpose*.

This is the foundation from which you'll lay a path specific to you. Trust me, this is going to be wonderful, and so much fun.

The student is ready. The teacher has appeared.

All that's left to do now is decide, believe and begin.

Decide…

Believe…

Begin…

Don't just read it. Don't just think it. *Do it*.

Decide.

Believe.

Begin.

Being a Top Performer starts today. Right now. Right this moment.

Decide!

Believe!

Begin!

· · ·

TASK

Make time.

Time and the lack of it is in the hall-of-fame of excuses. I don't have the time. I'll do it when I have time. I couldn't find the time. We've all gone to this well when we need to explain why we didn't take some action that would have made life better, happier and easier in the long term.

No more.

Make time.

I once had a boss who told me care is time spent. If you don't make time, you don't care enough. It's that simple. Figure out how much time it will take to pursue your goals, and set that time aside. If you need an hour, take an hour. If you need to, wake up earlier and stay up later. But make the time.

No excuses.

Time is precious, so spend it on what's most precious to you.

"*There is a difference between WISHING for a thing and being READY to receive it. No one is ready for a thing until he believes he can acquire it. The state of mind must be BELIEF, not mere hope or wish. Open-mindedness is essential for belief.*"

– Napoleon Hill

"*The world makes way for the man who knows where he is going.*"

– Ralph Waldo Emerson

Chapter 2
Attitude and Expectations

I promise you, everyone wants to be more, do more and have more. Everyone has positive wants. But few – far too few – have positive expectations. Put another way: everybody wants to succeed, but almost nobody expects to.

With the right attitude and expectation, the only thing between you and the attainment of your objectives is time.

Take a brief moment and think about yourself. Think about your own mind, your own life. Ask yourself…

How often do I expect excellent results?

How often do I expect the very best?

How often do I expect anything positive, spirit-enlarging and fun?

In my experience, most people's short and long term expectations are appallingly low. Most see their future as a string of hassles, grinds, and likely disappointments, with the odd happy day sprinkled in here and there.

I won't argue, as 'realists' often do, that what I just described is *real* life. That we are biologically predisposed toward dissatisfaction, reconciliation with sub-par circumstances and self-bargaining. Those things may be true.

But this isn't that kind of book.

Because what is also true – equally true, equally real! – is that human beings are sources of power, profound change and innovative aspiration. People are remarkable.

It requires incredible effort to settle. Settling for unhappiness exacts a spiritual tax, and even though living with that cost can feel like doing nothing, it's actually diligent labor to carry that pain, that weight of unexpressed wanting.

...

So why carry it?

Because you expect to. You *learned* to. Maybe those attitudes and expectations are something you acquired through bad experience or maybe you've had them so long you can't remember how, where, or when you picked them up.

Is it nature or nurture? Personally, I think there's a combination of both going on, at different volumes, all the time.

Nevertheless, I do believe most people are where they are to a large extent because of the environment and conditioning they grew up with.

But then we get older. We try something different, something bold and if it fails the first thing we do is say, "*I knew it...*" or "*Serves me right for...*" or "*That's the last time I...*" etc.

Think about this question for a moment –

Which is more important to you – developing self-acceptance or avoiding failure?

In my experience, most people say self-acceptance, but their *behavior* says otherwise. Avoiding failure and embarrassment, it seems to me, is one of the most dominant motivations in the day-to-day operations of the average person's life. In other words, most people denythe majority of their desires because they're afraid to risk individuality, have courage and gain genuine transcendence.

But believe me when I tell you:

Success, above all, is about being able to fail creatively without quitting. Successful people, Top Performers, fail all the time. They fail constantly, gloriously, creatively. With each failure, you should think to yourself –

What can I learn from this?

What can I improve?

It didn't work, but that doesn't mean it will never work. It just hasn't worked yet.

To fail creatively without quitting is to see each failure as another step on a stairway to success. Without the steps, there's no way up. But you must expect to go upwards; your *attitude* must be upward facing, or there can never be steps. Resilience is the ability to come back after great disappointment and pain, after great loss or failure... and still be truly alive.

And thus, if you don't put your *self*-worth before your *net* worth, the rewards will be hollow. It will all just be... *stuff.*

• • •

So, start saying your goodbyes now. Whatever negativity you're carrying around, you're about to begin the process of letting go. You won't need it where you're going. You won't miss it at all.

You can build a new expectation *starting today, right now*, by wrapping it around a beautiful desire, and then giving birth to that desire through activity. That activity – that action plan – we'll develop in this program as you go through it.

Just do it! is great advice... but just *do* what? To be a successful individual, you must do things in a certain way, not just *any way*. If you're to fulfill your dream of a better life, you must formulate a plan of action. Effective planning involves identifying and prioritizing those actions that will move you most efficiently toward what you want.

• • •

I set a personal vision back in February 1973.

At the time, I was successfully running my own equipment sales company. We were growing steadily; the future was promising and bright.

Moreover, I had become altogether... well, obsessed... with the field of personal development, and using universal laws to achieve goals. My mentor, the great Earl Nightingale, had inspired me and I wanted to inspire others. I had just begun speaking publicly and *knew*, with every molecule of my body, that this was what I wanted to do with my life.

I'd heard Bob Proctor speak, and I bought his personal empowerment tapes. I found him tremendously compelling and thought our styles would complement each other.

So, I went to work on a vision....

The vision I set was that I was to do full day seminars with Bob Proctor by February 1974. I had it written on a gold-colored card and I carried the card with me everywhere.

In the meantime, my speaking career continued to gain steam. I was meeting my goals at a steady rate, working hard at the craft of moving and motivating people and helping them realize and meet their potential. I had absolutely no doubt that my vision would come true and *absolutely no idea how it would.*

(*This is important: when pursuing your goals, visions and purpose, do the work and let the universe take care of the how.*)

Well 1974 came around, and one day I was out on my snowmobile with my wife, having a good old time near Ontario. Out of nowhere a friend tracked us down, coming toward us across the snow.

My friend said, "Bob Proctor has been looking for you. He's been calling around to different people from the seminars wondering if he can get a hold of you."

Interesting, I thought…

So, we drove to my friend's house and I called Bob.

"How are you doing, Bob?"

And Bob said –

"John, I'm in Chicago and I'm snowed in. I won't be able to get out of here in time to speak in Toronto tomorrow. I hear terrific things about you and wondered if you could get down there and fill in for me."

This was February 24th, 1974.

I got to that seminar and wound up working with Bob Proctor for over 25 years. It's one of the greatest relationships of my life. We remain friends to this day.

Was I nervous, standing in front of that crowd in Toronto?

Of course!

But it was a good kind of nervous. It was the splendid nervousness of knowing *This is the moment! This is what you've worked for.*

At no point on that stage, or on the ride over, or on the snowmobile the day before, or during the year leading up to it, did I expect anything less than the actualization of what I had set out to do.

I changed my attitude, I set my expectations, I worked my tail off to meet my goals and the world moved to meet me. The world was ready all along.

You might say to me – as many have – that Bob's calling me that February day was nothing more than luck. And maybe you're right.

But what is luck?

The Roman philosopher Seneca wrote –

Luck is what happens when preparation meets opportunity.

Luck is everywhere, all around, lying in wait for the prepared mind. Perhaps my example is particularly specific and potent, but the lesson remains: I did everything in my ability to put myself in the path of opportunity, to recognize it when it was coming. So, when opportunity came, I saw it for what it was, accepted it unquestioningly and unconditionally, and seized it.

The best luck in the world can come along, and it will pass you by if you're not ready. It will evaporate or move on to someone else, someone who is ready.

For a more contemporary definition of luck, we can look to the baseball manager Branch Rickey, who said –

Luck is the residue of design.

Walk a road of achievement, and you'll be shocked at how lucky you get.

By the way, the vision on my card was this:

I am so grateful to speak and teach a prosperity seminar with Bob Proctor by February 1974. I help others reach joy and prosperity by speaking and living with passion and a full heart.

So yes, I was lucky.

And being that lucky is hard work.

• • •

But remember! None of this will happen without your *attitude* and *expectations* being in order first. Believe, know, without a doubt, that you can do this. You will meet your goals, achieve your visions and live your purpose. Being *interested* is not enough; interest is not *commitment*. You must be so committed that all obstacles appear as minor irritations.

As I mentioned earlier, when used properly, attitude, expectations and activity – negative or positive – align you with the harmonious vibrations of universal attraction. You will get what you put out.

Put out junk, get junk back. Put out beauty, receive beauty in return. You can be sure of it. It's universal law.

Living well is not one thing, but many things working harmonically together. With a clear first vision and truly, deeply positive attitude and expectations, you have your first note.

Now, let's turn that note into music.

• • •

TASK

We're going to set a vision.

We'll call it your **First Vision**.

Get a blank page or note card and write "First Vision" at the top.

Now…

Think about something you want.

Something you want to achieve, to create, to be, with all your heart.

Something that will take the surpassing of multiple goals to bring to reality.

Something that gives you chills, that makes your entire being smile, when you think about it.

Write it down.

Be sure to write the present tense!

I am a [YOUR VISION].
or
I have [YOUR VISION].
or
I am so grateful to be [YOUR VISION].
or
I am so grateful to have [YOUR VISION].

This reflective writing is a necessary step. Writing is talking on paper and seeing what you think.

So, write your vision. Declare it.

This is the outset of making your dreams into something real in the material world. You are turning your first vision into a tangible thing.

Writing creates thinking. Thinking creates an image. Images create feelings. Feelings create an action. For every action there is a reaction. Thus, you make writing the first step in a chain of actions.

Say your first vision out loud.

Say it without doubt.

Say it loud enough for your soul to hear it.

Say it until you know you are speaking the Truth.

"I say unto you, what things so ever ye desire, when ye pray, believe that ye receive them, and ye shall have them."
– Mark 11:24

"Ample make this bed. Make this bed with awe."
– Emily Dickinson

Chapter 3

Goals

Goals are the short-term things we do in order to achieve visions.

Goals are strategic: They have clear, finite ends. *They are not vague.*

But goals are also deeply aspirational. They defy the past. They challenge us to exceed what we have done before, and force us to *quantify* what it will take to be the Top Performer we imagine ourselves becoming. Powerful goals that you love to achieve make for a powerful life.

A goal should be thrilling and a little scary at the outset. Like starting a great hike, you look into the distance, at the trail winding up... up... up... to a far-off peak. And part of you thinks – *it's much easier to stay down here; I'm safe down here; I can't fail if I stay down here...*

But a larger and louder part thinks – *I can't wait to see what the world looks like from there!*

And then you start climbing.

...

This next quality might seem obvious, but many get it wrong.

It's critical that your goals are authentic to you!

They must be your goals, produced by honest reflection on the life you desire. After all, goals are the products of an *individual* creative process.

Earlier today, I had a phone call with a new client in Alberta, Canada. For a while, she's had the goal of becoming a regional director with the company she works for. She's been chipping away at this goal for a long time, she says, but never quite makes it. She's growing frustrated, aware that her approach is ineffective, but she can't see a solution.

I asked about her attitudes and expectations. Both are positive. She works hard. She's driven and kind. I believe she's a person who will eventually achieve what she's set out to do. And then I asked –

"Why do you want to be a regional director?"

She searched for an answer that wouldn't come. Eventually she said it's for the prestige.

I told her she can have prestige whether she's a regional director or not. "What else?"

She said it's for the extra money.

I told her she can earn more money whether she's a regional director or not. "What else?"

Turns out she had no idea why she wants to be a regional director. She didn't have any sense of an overriding vision or purpose in her life. She didn't even find the job particularly appealing. What she has, when we got to the core of it, is a goal without a foundation.

So I recommended she set aside some time to get very honest with herself. Decide what, more than anything else, she really wants to do, to have, to be. I told her to write it down. All of it. Don't get fancy. Don't try to show off and display how smart you are. Just let yourself relax. Speak to yourself in the plainest language possible.

Don't consult anyone at first – this is a moment for the Self to consult with *itself*. This is a time for self-reflection and revelation.

I have a feeling her objectives will soon change. Don't you?

The point is that some people's goals are shockingly distant from what they ought to be doing. They think *any* goal will do.

Or – like ingrained biases and opinions – their objectives were acquired early on, and have survived the years without revisiting or renovation.

Know this: Any goal will *not* do.

Think for a moment about your current goals.

Where did they come from?

Do they move you toward your visions? Are they the conduits through which you live a purpose?

Do you *really* want them? Do you really want that career, that apartment, that etc. etc., or are you performing karaoke for someone else's image of a fulfilling life?

Don't kid yourself: Goals are labor. Chip away at them, and you'll succeed. You can create a life that represents who you are, or you can create the opposite.

What will your life be?

What future are your goals building?

...

Which brings us to goal types.

In becoming a Top Performer, it's necessary to set the right kinds of goals, or you'll just perpetuate the same patterns, the same results, over and over.

There are three primary goal types, which we'll call A, B, and C goals. These can be broadly described as follows –

AGOALS
What you *know* you can do.

AGoals are things you have done before and can reliably do again. (*i.e. I earned X amount of money last year; I will try to earn that same amount this year.*) Top Performers steer clear of AGoals because they make a habit of constantly *reevaluating* what they're capable of. Top Performers separate themselves from patterns that yield unsatisfactory results. Your spirit is meant for the business of excellence and delight. AGoals keep you running in place. Avoid them.

BGOALS
What you *think* you can do.

BGoals are aspiration without purpose. They are positive because they employ the imagination and help you attain newer, higher standards. BGoals force you to strategize and expect overachievement. However, BGoals are ultimately empty, because they aren't infused with a *higher* meaning. They're not specific to the person who has them. BGoals build useful habits, but they shouldn't become a way of life. (My aforementioned client's goal of being a regional director, for instance, is a typical BGoal).

C GOALS
What you *want*.

C Goals are where goals meet purpose. C Goals are outlandish dreams, moonshots. They keep you awake at night. You smile when you think about them. Almost all your goals should be some variety of CGoal. The best part about CGoals is that they force you to *visualize* your dreams with *specificity*, and thereby alter your real live circumstances. *They require fantasy!* Create an image in your mind; your internal vibration changes; a whole new constellation of things becomes attracted to you. CGoals are the daily currency of the Top Performer.

. . .

Here's a CGoal story of mine –

I used to do sales for Prudential. I was working out of Illinois at the time, and one day I got a call from the president of the Mid-America region.

"John," he said, "I just got this memo on the seminar you're doing, and I love this campaign objective you have of five million dollars a week."

I almost fell off the chair.

There was a typo in the memo. I'd meant to say five million dollars a *month!*

But I wasn't about to call my boss back and tell him the mistake.

I sat down and thought it through…

And I realized…

If I truly believe what I say about the power of goals and expectations, who cares about the dollar amount? If a 5 million dollar week is the strategic goal that moves me toward my vision, then so be it. Scale is no matter. That's where I'll direct all of myself. That's what I choose to imagine.

We made $10 million in the first week.

. . .

It's a tremendous advantage to *know what kind of goal you're pursuing at any given time.* Know when you have identified an A, B or C Goal; know which objectives are serving you well or poorly, which hold you back and which propel you forward.

Soon – probably sooner than expected – you're going to find that not only will your results improve, but that improvement is exponential and sustainable.

· · ·

Finally, we must talk about accountability and responsibility.

Ralph Waldo Emerson, who I quoted at the beginning of this chapter, put it very well when he said:

> *"Of what use to make heroic vows of amendment if the same old lawbreaker is to keep them?"*

That just makes a whole lot of sense, doesn't it? We make promises to ourselves, but do we keep them? And what's the point of those promises – of what use are they if they're consistently broken or abandoned before fulfillment?

I believe every Top Performer knows that prosperity begins by taking responsibility for the outcomes you want, whether they be personal (yourself), interpersonal (your relationships), or material (your things).

Goals don't just move you toward your long term visions, they hold you *accountable* to them. If there are things we want to do in our lives, the first requirement is taking responsibility for *doing* the things that will lead us to personal freedom. Life, liberty, and the pursuit of happiness. Think about it. There's a reason, I believe, the *pursuit of happiness* is so closely linked to *liberty*. Liberty – another word for freedom – is a necessary effect of working toward one's goals, and vice versa.

Goals exist to be done. To be *accomplished*. To be achieved and moved on from. It's never enough to want. Wanting is free and lasts forever. Wanting alone (or visions and purpose alone) will get you nowhere.

Thomas Edison – no slouch as a Top Performer himself – wisely observed that, "*Opportunity is missed by most people because it is dressed in overalls and looks like work.*"

That's what goals are: potential glory dressed in overalls.

And so, in assessing whether or not you're really pursuing your goals, be compassionately ruthless with yourself. Be your harshest *and* most loving critic. Find power in the little things in life; from them is drawn the power to create life's greatest gifts.

· · ·

Because in the long run, it turns out it's not easier to stay put.

Your life *will* happen. Time will pass. Opportunities don't go *away*, they go to *someone* else.

So, choose a destination.

Set a course.

Don't fear the work.

Change is inevitable. Growth is optional.

Take that first step…

… then the next… then the next…

You won't believe what the world looks like from up there.

· · ·

TASK

Make a list.

What are 5 things you can do to achieve your First Vision?

What will it take? What will it take first?

What could you do right now, if you wanted?

And if you're stuck (i.e. if you don't know what it will take, and don't know what you can do) –

Has your vision ever been achieved before?

Who has done it? Who has inspired your vision, or the pieces of it?

Reach out to them. Try to get in touch.

What did they do? How did they create their results? What about their process can you replicate?

Now you have your strategy, and you have your goals.

Do them all. And when you're done, make another list.

And another… and another….

"Worse than being blind is having sight but no vision."
– Helen Keller

"Seize this very minute!
What you can do, or think you can, begin it!
Only engage, and then the mind grows heated;
Begin it, and the work will be completed."
– Johan Wolfgang von Goethe/John Anster

CHAPTER 4
VISIONS

The Top Performer is always learning and changing, comfortable in a grateful state of *becoming*.

What will you become?

Your visions are what you will become.

And what will you become after?

You'll move on to new visions.

The Top Performer is never a finished product.

. . .

Goals are practical and schematic (your purpose broken down to manageable steps).Purpose is radically unattainable (the divine carrot on the stick, in a never-ending and forever rewarding chase.)Visions fall somewhere in between.

Visions are goals, but larger…

Or purpose, but smaller…

They require definition while simultaneously transcending their own defined boundaries. They are predictions of the unpredictable, containers for the uncontainable, diaries *and* blueprints.

. . .

At the most basic level, visions are the result of achieving goals. You start somewhere, you go somewhere. If I set and accomplish enough goals, it stands to reason that eventually, I'll reach my vision(s).

This is a mostly serviceable definition. In fact, when I'm working with a new client, the rule of thumb I use to separate visions and goals is based on this very model: *Cause and effect over time.*

So if you're feeling stuck setting your vision(s), here's an easy way to begin. Ask yourself:

If I meet my goals –

Where will I be in 1 year?

Where will I be in 3 years?

Where will I be in 10 years?

The answer to each of the above questions, if excavated well, is a Vision.

You can and should repeat this process for multiple areas of life. For starters, as a Top Performer, what are your relationships like? Friendships, marriages, relationships between parents and children – these are tremendous achievements (possibly the most important kind!). In your visions, who do you love and how do you show it? Who gets your quality time? By what ways and means will you enhance, improve, and expand the relationships you care about?

Just as we can pursue several goals simultaneously, the Top Performer can pursue multiple visions at once. You can cast a wide net as long as you give equal passion and focus to everything it falls on. Ask yourself:

If I meet my Goals –

Where will I be spiritually?

Where will I be professionally?

Where will I live?

Honestly answer these questions. Jot down some ideas about how you want to live as a Top Performer. Soon you'll see the outlines of a life – your life – take shape.

Make a projected inventory based on the attainment of your Goals. See it. *Emotionally* invest in it. Give your energy to it. The life you're aiming for is entirely possible.

· · ·

But don't stop there. Keep thinking, keep imagining. More, more, more!

This is the place where goals and visions diverge...

It isn't so simple as an equation: *Goal + Goal + Goal = Vision*.

The best visions require more than math.

Know this: A vision is not made good or useful just by being itself, just as all art isn't good art, just because it's art. A Vision is a noun – like a car, house or flower – without intrinsic value.

So, what makes a good vision?

. . .

In his poem *The Third Thing*, D.H. Lawrence writes –

> *Water is H2O, hydrogen two parts, oxygen one,*
> *but there is also a third thing, that makes it water*
> *and nobody knows what it is.*

The strongest visions, I have found, possess that mystical 'other' ingredient. They have goals and time (deadlines) and then another thing:Some magic sparkle that turns them into meaningful visions. They have it. They have the third thing.

Consider your First Vision, for instance. It's the fulfillment of your goals, of course, but isn't it, somehow, more? It *feels* a certain way, right? When you imagine it, it feels almost as if you're peering into an alternate dimension, doesn't it? And in this dimension, you're almost, but not entirely the same, aren't you? It's different than what happens when you imagine the achievement of a goal. It's nice to imagine quitting smoking or remodeling a kitchen or starting a savings account, but imagining those things doesn't seem to send an electric current through the air. Visions do that. Visions have the buzz.

. . .

How do we know quality visions when we see them? Well... we kind of don't. It requires trial and error, even failure. This logic can be frustratingly circular at first –

Your lasting visions will be the ones that last.

Your enduring visions will be the ones that endure.

Your best visions are the ones that win.

But the process works. It just does. The Top Performer must learn to accept the mysteries inherent in the refinement and distillation of goals, visions and purpose. Life, when lived to the fullest, is an incredible editor.

That said, I also can say the following...

• • •

The visions I have seen last longest and work best – in my life and the lives of my clients – are profoundly, uncompromisingly personal. They are attempts to express the hopes and dreams of an individual. One person. The only *you* who has ever existed.

Which is why I believe it's so important to be highly specific about the words we use when speaking and writing our visions. I can't stress this enough. It's so important.

Now you might say, *fair enough John, but how do I find those words?*

Well, in order to wrap the right words around your visions, you'll need to access your *creative speech.*

• • •

In his writings on the origins and nature of language, the philosopher Maurice Merleau-Ponty draws a distinction between ordinary speech (or *empirical* speech) and creative speech (or *authentic/true* speech)

In short, ordinary speech is the system of commonly held understandings and meanings that makes everyday conversation possible. Most of our speech is ordinary speech.

So, let's say *Person A* and *Person B* are old acquaintances who run into each other on the street –

Person A
Good morning.

Person B
Hey, nice to see you.

Person A
Likewise. How have you been?

Person B
Great. No complaints. Yourself?

Person A
Fine. Same old same old.

Person B
Glad to hear it… well I should take off. I'm late for a lunch.

Person A
Of course, yeah. Nice running into you.

Person B
You too. Take care.

This is a typical exchange of ordinary speech. Perfectly pleasant and useful, totally adequate to its purpose.

But certainly not introspective, searching, inspiring, or revelatory. Revelation is not what ordinary speech is *for*.

That's what creative speech is for.

And creative speech is the domain of visions.

• • •

Of creative speech Merleau-Ponty writes –

"Language signifies when instead of copying thought, it lets itself be taken apart and put together again by thought. Language bears the sense of thought as a footprint signifies the movement and effort of a body."

In other words, your thoughts *transform* and take on a new *life* when fed through the filter of creative speech. Creative speech uses the toolbox of language to bring into being something new, something altogether singular.

Feelings are powerful and enormously important, but it isn't enough to feel visions.

So many people are trying desperately to create a new life by holding on to old ideas, and that includes using lazy language to define their dreams. Stop that!

What do you want most? What do you desire most?

Visions, when they work, are the Self speaking to the Self, mentoring the Self, giving direction to the Self. I suppose the simplest way to say it is this:

The best visions have *soul*.

...

I already told you the story of how I began working with Bob Proctor – the vision card, the call on the snowmobile and speech in Toronto on a moment's notice.

What I didn't tell you was that I had not anticipated any of what happened after. I had imagined myself working with Bob a thousand times, but it never occurred to me we might become long-time friends, or that we would develop the *Born Rich* program together. Or, that as I learned from him, he might learn from me, too. Those realities exceeded my imagination and my imagination had to catch up.

My visions changed as my experience of the world changed, and my new and old visions were forced to take these new experiences into account. I was learning and applying new knowledge to old precedents.

The message here is that visions are fluid. You pursue them whole-heartedly, even stubbornly, but not stupidly, don't ignore what you learn on the journey.

As visions are an expression of self, it follows they'll grow and mature with you.

...

When focusing on your visions, when speaking them, and especially when writing them down, give yourself time. Let yourself really think about the elements fundamental to their composition.

Love

Happiness

Abundance

God

Home

Family

Career

Peace

Security

Nature

What do these words mean to you? How would you describe their presence and practice in your life? In order to know this, you must make an effort to know yourself, and to put these desires into words, you must speak *authentically*.

Quiet yourself, humble yourself...

Don't judge. Don't focus on *good*. Focus on *honest*.

In turning dreams into words...

And words into matter...

The words matter.

Think your visions in your language. Write your visions in *your* language. Then live your visions in your language.

. . .

TASK

Set 5 minutes aside every day to meditate on your First Vision.

(I prefer mornings, but any time will do)

Think about it in the finest, most granular detail. Hold the vision in your mind and explore it, see it. What's it like? What's your vision made of?

For example, let's say you have a vision to open your own restaurant, and your first Vision is opening for your first day of business –

What color are the walls?

What's on the menu?

How heavy is the door when you turn your key in the lock and open it?

Where is your restaurant located?

How many staff?

Is there music playing?

What is the smell of the food cooking?

The point of this imaginative practice is to put yourself on the same vibration as your First Vision, so that you're creating it in the world, and attracting to yourself the people and things required to achieve it.

Spend time in your First Vision every day. Imagine boldly. Piece by piece, you'll find your life changing as you do the work required to turn your imagination into reality.

"*Nothing will work unless you do.*"
– Maya Angelou

"*I dream my painting and I paint my dream.*"
– Vincent Van Gogh

CHAPTER 5

PURPOSE

In the Gospel of John, we're told that Jesus Christ, after restoring the sight of a blind man, spoke to the Pharisees about His work on earth, and the task of the Good Shepherd. "*The thief cometh not but for to steal, and to kill, and to destroy*," He said. And then this:

I am come that they might have life,
and that they might have it more abundantly.

– John 10:10

Such a profound thought. I have read it thousands and thousands of times and never tire of it.

Whatever your background is, whichever God you believe in – whether or not you believe in the Divine at all – I encourage you to hold this quote as an exquisite, powerful example of someone declaring their life's purpose.

The Top Performer, likewise, has a purpose that manifests in all aspects of their being. Every action the Top Performer takes is, to one degree or another, an extension of their core purpose.

But of what stuff is that word made for the Top Performer? When we say purpose, what do we *mean*? In the most basic terms –

Purpose is what the story of your life is about.

Purpose is your big *Why*.

Remember the Achievement Pyramid? There is a reason why Purpose sits at the very top. It's the height to which you are always climbing, striving, ascending. It's the endless work that yields endless joys.

More practically, purpose is the animating principle of your visions and goals. In the metaphysical chain of command, visions and goals report directly to purpose. Purpose is their boss. It always knows best.

Yet, as I constantly remind my clients (And myself!), one's purpose is often mysterious. It's conceptually difficult to separate from visions and goals and, once separated, can be even more difficult to articulate in a way that's *useful*. This process can be especially frustrating because the feeling of being drawn toward your purpose is so strong. Every cell of your body is tuned to a hidden frequency, but when asked the most basic and reasonable question, *WHAT DO YOU WANT?*... the... words...just... won't... come.

I think of the Steven Spielberg film *Close Encounters of the Third Kind*. The character Roy, played by Richard Dreyfuss, sees an alien spacecraft one night, and from then on, he's obsessed with something he can't name. Roy feels called, chosen. He looks at the stars. He looks at maps. He builds models with houseplants and dirt and piles of mashed potatoes, repeating the same words: "This means something. This is important."

You don't need to see a UFO to have this feeling. Many on the threshold of revelation have felt it. Maybe you're feeling it too. Something is there. *Something means something. Something is important.*

Don't worry. We'll find it.

I am come that they might have life, and that they might have it more abundantly.

Poetic, isn't it? And, let's be honest, abstract. What does it mean to "have life"? Is it simply *being alive?* Or is having life something more than the biological fact of being alive? And what is it to live abundantly? My abundance might not resemble your abundance, to say nothing of my neighbor's abundance, and their neighbor's, etc.

But the line's abstraction is deceiving...

Because despite all that's up for interpretation, I believe these words also contain profound focus and overwhelming rigor. Moreover, I see a clear-eyed commitment to humanity and service. You would never read this and think the person who spoke it wanted people to be unhappy, unfulfilled, stuck. There's generosity of spirit and magnificent intent here. This purpose, if acted upon, is driving inevitably toward a common good.

Here again is how I, John Kanary, define my purpose – (I hope you'll indulge my writing for being a step down from the Gospel of John…)

Create as many exceptional leaders as I possibly can, and empower them to duplicate that process by creating new leaders in their own communities.

This is what I stand for. It's why I do the things I do. My goals and visions aspire to it.

Again I call your attention to its nebulous quality – What does it mean to be a good leader? How, specifically, do you create leaders and make sure they create leaders in return? How do you pay rent? What do you do with your time? – combined with unshakeable commitment to love and service. Purpose is about other people as much as it is about the self. When living your purpose only benefits you, you are doing it wrong!

Finally, try to keep it short. If you can't speak your purpose in a few sentences or less, you probably haven't found it yet. Don't worry if this is difficult at first. You'll get plenty of practice speaking and refining your purpose with your Mastermind Group (more on that in Mastermind Chapter.)

Because this is such a foundational concept, I want to take a moment to hone in on what distinguishes purpose from the other categories of pursuit.

Consider the following –

Historian and theological scholar James P. Carse writes about varieties of human endeavor in his book *Finite and Infinite Games*. In defining his two types of games, Carse writes –

"*A finite game is played for the purpose of winning, an infinite game for the purpose of continuing the play.*"

This is also a useful way to think about the difference between purpose, goals and visions.

Visions, and especially goals, are finite games. They have boundaries. When pursuing them, you can measure your progress. You can keep score. You can win. You can lose.

A: I will lose 50 pounds and open my own gym.

B: I will have three kids.

C: I will be a millionaire.

D: I will start a charity for clean drinking water in impoverished areas.

These are goals, or perhaps visions, but they are not purpose.

Purpose is an infinite game.

Your Purpose is a game to be played without the aim of winning, or fear of losing. *Purpose is a way to live, not a thing to do.* You're either living your purpose, or living outside of it. For the individual, purpose is the ultimate infinite game. Its beauty *is* its infinity.

> A: *I radiate health and dedicate myself to helping others live healthy lives.*
>
> B: *I will be a great parent and make the world better by raising compassionate, ambitious children.*
>
> C: *Prosperity and wealth are my state of being. I am wealthy inside and out, and the people in my life experience me as an embodiment of generosity, humility, and grace.*
>
> D: *I will improve the world by creating access to life, education and opportunity wherever I can.*

This is purpose.

Are you following so far?

Mastery is an infinite game. Fulfillment is an infinite game. Your purpose is never finished. Your purpose is your art. You wouldn't be you without it.

When I need an inspiring example of the endurance and longevity of true purpose, I often look to the life of Nelson Mandela.

A lawyer and renowned activist, Mandela was imprisoned in 1963 for his work in opposition to the Dutch occupation of his native South Africa. Over the next 27 years of his incarceration, he continued to study and write, refusing numerous conditional offers for release, never renouncing the statements he made during his trial decades earlier –

> *"I have fought against white domination, and I have fought against black domination. I have cherished the ideal of a democratic and free society in which all persons live together in harmony and with equal opportunities. It is an ideal which I hope to live for and to achieve. But if needs be, it is an ideal for which I am prepared to die."*

Mandela was released from prison in 1990 and became his country's first democratically elected president four years later. After leaving office he continued to speak and work for humanitarian causes.

In this life we see an unbroken narrative of someone living their purpose, through thick and thin. Purpose, it would seem, helped Nelson Mandela to endure and transcend circumstances that might have proved unbearable without it. He died in 2013 at the age of 95.

With a life like that, I'd bet he still felt there was much more work to do. And I'd bet again that he would've been excited to do it. Don't you agree?

Because if you've had enough of fulfilling your purpose, you have the wrong purpose in mind.

I don't stop being hungry today because I ate yesterday. Hunger is a renewable resource. Likewise with purpose. There's never enough. You can always have another helping of it tomorrow. You will scour life's fridge for more and more and more purpose.

So ask yourself – what gives meaning and value to your life? *Meaning and value.*

What's the game you love to play – and play and play! – without end? Rest assured the game we call purpose can *only* be played. Moreover, and hold this close: *Your* purpose is a game that can only be played by you.

Before moving on, let's return briefly to James Carse, and this resonant passage on the infinite game of gardening.

"Gardening is not outcome-oriented. A successful harvest is not the end of a gardener's existence, but only a phase of it. As any gardener knows, the vitality of a garden does not end with a harvest. It simply takes another form. Gardens do not "die' in the winter but quietly prepare for another season."

What, or where, or who, is the 'garden' in your life? How much time do you spend there, and are you tending it well?

If not, what are you waiting for?

Go. Go go go.

Your garden is waiting for you. Your purpose is waiting for you.

This means something. This is important.

Have life, and have it abundantly.

$\bullet \bullet \bullet$

TASK

When were you happiest?

What are the best times of your life?

Think about – write down – some of your happiest memories. Think about the moments you have felt most fulfilled, most of service, most at ease in your own mind and spirit and skin.

What do these times have in common?

We have established how purpose can be elusive and resist articulation. Be that as it may, it's always useful to reflect upon. In my experience, one's sense of inner peace is always in direct relation to how closely they are living their purpose.

As you consider these happy memories, take care not to get lost in surface details. Purpose is the intention (whether conscious or subconscious) behind actions, but rarely can purpose be easily read in the actions themselves.

For example, someone whose purpose is raising a beautiful family might find transcendent happiness in a million seemingly-unrelated events and tasks, because that's the everyday matter of raising a family. It would require the excavation of this deeper intention and source of meaning to realize that it's family, not the tasks and events alone, that is the source of this feeling.

And finally: Be patient.

Purpose is a long game. You don't need to be in any hurry to speak it. Be intentional. Be authentic. But don't rush.

"If I knew you and you knew me,
If both of us could clearly see,
And with an inner sight divine,
The meaning of your heart and mine,
I'm sure that we would differ less,
And clasp our hands in friendliness;
Our thoughts would pleasantly agree,
If I knew you and you knew me."

– Anonymous

"When we speak we are afraid our words will not be
heard or welcomed. But when we are silent, we are still afraid.
So it is better to speak."

– Audre Lorde

Chapter 6
Effective Communication

The next two Chapters will focus on sales – the methods and techniques a Top Performer uses to be effective and prosperous in even the most competitive marketplace.

To all readers pursuing a sales career, the value of these chapters will be obvious. But of course, not everyone shares those aspirations.

And so, if you're going through this book for other reasons, you might be tempted to skip ahead. You might be thinking, *What does this have to do with me?*

The answer:

Plenty! Don't skip ahead!!

Sales are a dynamic, enormously useful metaphor for life and how to live it well. The lessons and exercises detailed in these chapters will prove invaluable in all walks of life.

. . .

Consider –

At heart, all sales are transactions of desire. *I want. You want. What do we both want and how can we collaborate to get it?*

We all play the role of buyer and seller on a daily basis; we constantly participate in transactions, large and small.

Convincing, persuading, negotiating, bargaining… these are all versions of selling.

Considering, compromising, saying yes, saying maybe… these are all versions of buying.

A good sale is beneficial both parties, and so it follows that the Top Performer is always interested and emotionally invested in the prospect/client, what they want and how to serve them. (Remember: this dedication to service is an extension and outgrowth of purpose.).

. . .

Let's look again at the title of this Chapter: *Effective Communication*.

Webster's Dictionary defines the words *Effective* and *Communication* as follows:

Effective –

1 a : producing a decided, decisive or desired effect.

Communication–

1 a : a process by which information is exchanged between individuals through a common system of symbols, signs or behavior

Taken together, we can define Effective Communication for the Top Performer as –

A process of exchanging information in order to produce a decisive or desired effect.

Put another way, we want to develop the conscious awareness of how to build a connecting passage between ourselves and another individual or groups of individuals, so that images and intentions can be transferred from our minds to theirs, and likewise their minds to ours, in an efficient or powerful manner.

That lines up extremely well with goals, visions and purpose, doesn't it?

Effective Communication, therefore, is absolutely essential to the Top Performer.

. . .

In one of his final works, Ralph Waldo Emerson wrote –

Don't say things. What you are stands over you the while, and thunders so that I cannot hear what you say to the contrary.

Over time, this quotation has been and distilled down to the more famous –

What you are speaks so loudly I cannot hear what you say.

Whichever version you prefer, the meaning holds: *Communication is holistic.* If a person is speaking, but their words do not match their presence, the words are meaningless. Words are a physical expression of something much deeper.

. . .

Unfortunately, a lot of people believe they can only they communicate by talking. Actually, we communicate on three different levels: the intellectual, the emotional/spiritual, and the physical.

Among the greatest problems in life is the lack or malfunctioning of communications. Too frequently, what a person is saying is not in sync with what they're *thinking*, and what they're *saying and thinking* is not in harmony with what they're *doing*.

How often have you had this experience?

When a person has all three elements – intellectual, emotional, physical – lined up and moving in accord, we refer to that as integrity. Integrity is indispensable to a Top Performer's long term fulfillment and prosperity.

. . .

We are all interdependent beings. People want to feel connected. They can do it in love, in prayer, in service or in production. In any case, you simply can't function in a truly dynamic, creative and excellent state by yourself. You need other people.

Effective communication is not merely something to be desired to improve the relationships in your life; effective communication is an absolute prerequisite for success in every human undertaking.

When it becomes a habit to get other people what they want in life, the Law of Cause and Effect will see to it that other people become the medium through which good will is delivered to you. Mind you, the people you help might not be the medium(s) through which your good comes, but come it will. Come it must.

In short: It's impossible to improve oneself without also improving the lives of others.

. . .

So what, in particular, are Top Performers *like* in their sales encounters? What do they *do*? And most of all, how might we practice sales as an extension of our most important and enduring values?

Here are 10 rules the Top Performer can follow to become a more effective communicator:

I

Ask questions and listen intently.

Meaningful talking is about sharing, and meaningful listening is about caring.

When meeting with a prospect, it's vitally important to ask the right questions, then listen carefully to the answers, because our *real* objective in doing so is to form a *composite*. Where is the place our two objectives meet and how can we get there? Ultimately, we want to march in the same direction together.

By asking questions, I'm going to find out what's important to the prospect. I just can't project my idea(s) of what's important onto them. What do they want? Where do they want to go in life?

If I don't then supplement my attentive asking with attentive *listening*, I'm going to miss the message. There's a big difference between *hearing* and *listening*. We hear with our ears, but we listen with our emotions.

You might not always get the answers you expect or want, but without listening, you'll never be able to lead the prospect in a direction that will improve their quality of life.

II

Increase the prospect's self-esteem.

When building this composite, the whole idea is to get the other person to feel good, to be excited and optimistic. It's also necessary those good feelings be connected to *you*, *your* products, *your* services. This is the focus of a Top performer's attention.

In other words, the prospect feels better about themselves the closer they move to the destination you've set.

III

Call your Prospect by name often.

Speaking someone's name is an important aspect of creating personal connection. Names indicate specificity, memory, and history.

Remembering names isn't easy for everyone, and not everyone's memory functions the same way.

If you struggle to remember names, **work to get better!**

There are many techniques that can help, and many books on the subject. I recommend starting with the names section of "The Memory Book" by Harry Lorayne and Jerry Lucas. If that doesn't work for you, find something that does. Practice. You'll get good at it.

IV
Expect the results you want.

This goes back to attitude and expectations. Your mindset is directly related to your vibration, and your vibration is directly related to what you attract to yourself (Law of Attraction). The Top Performer is always operating in a positive state, and therefore attracting positive results in return.

When meeting a prospect, your expectation is what you're thinking, pushed to the forefront of your awareness (though it's not always what you're saying) so that you're transmitting the necessary vibrations on a subconscious level. Ineffective communication can almost always be traced back to negative expectations. Choose to live in a world of "Yes."

V
Harness your criticism.

This is so, so important!

Nobody's perfect.

Nobody gets what they want all the time.

The important thing is that we *use* our criticism as fuel to *improve*. Don't hold on to it. If you dwell too long on criticism, it becomes toxic. You'll never establish a meaningful relationship with a prospect if you're sending bad energy their way. Criticism is not a problem, it's an opportunity to get better, quickly.

VI
Project confidence.

I don't believe a person will ever sell anything without a confident bearing.

Imagine going in for a risky operation, and the doctor saying "I hope this works." You'd jump off the table and run as fast as possible to another hospital.

It's exactly the same when you're making a sale. Top Performers project confidence. Not arrogance – confidence. Bob Proctor always says *confidence is strength with style.*

Be good. Be useful. Be excellent. Be essential.

Know it. Enjoy it.

That's confidence.

VII
Be direct.

Top performers are very direct. They avoid being vague, misleading or withholding.

Some people think if you're too direct you'll scare people away, that you're being arrogant or overbearing.

No.

Directness is honesty without arrogance.

When meeting a prospect, directness is the only way to effectively communicate. People appreciate you being candid. You can have candor and kindness at the same time.

VIII
Be sincere.

Sincerity is similar to integrity.

It's having your thoughts, feelings and actions aligned. Say what you mean and mean what you say.

You can be funny and still remain sincere.

You can even be sarcastic and still remain sincere.

But you can't be fake or dishonest and still remain sincere.

Sincerity can be vulnerable, and vulnerability can be scary. But Top Performers face this fear and are willing to risk being vulnerable.

Integrity, authenticity and sincerity are all neighbors.

IX
Be friendly.

This is a natural result of following Rules I-VIII.

Wouldn't you agree the best friendships are based on listening, vulnerability, compromise, sincerity, directness and trust?

It follows, then, that Top Performers are able to turn our prospects into clients and clients into friends. Not all prospects will turn out this way, but some certainly will.

And while you shouldn't have friendship as a goal when you're selling, it can be useful for Top Performers to hold themselves accountable to this question:

Is this how I would treat a friend?

X

Be a good-finder.

The businessman and author W. Clement Stone was fond of saying, "That's good." It didn't matter what happened, he'd still say "That's good."

Everything has an opposite. Whatever you look at, there is good and bad, positive and negative, inside it. Look for the good and you'll find it. Find the good in success, and especially find the good in failure. (*Remember: Success is the ability to fail creatively without quitting!*)

. . .

Norman Vincent Peale said something that beautifully summarizes what we just covered:

> *"I see salesmanship as a process of persuasion whereby another individual is induced to walk the road of agreement with you."*

Selling, like all of life's richest relationships, is pastoral. People walk together. People find common ground. People gain independence and interdependence through shared choices.

Practice with dedication these fundamentals of communication. Maintain and improve them every day, whenever you can, as much as you can.

As your relationships improve, and as your mind, spirit and body align, you'll find selling requires less and less effort. Selling will be natural. Selling will be fun. Selling will be easy.

I tell my clients to think of effective communication and sales like a building a campfire –

If you want the fire, you can't stare at the firewood and say "Give me the heat. I command you! Give me the heat!"

You have to help it and work it. You have to kneel on the ground with your kindling, create a space protected from wind, a small corner where heat has a chance to exist at all. You have to blow on the kindling and create friction and nurse the flame from its tiniest spark, when it's so delicate a breath could extinguish it altogether.

The heat is there, within the firewood. But it only comes as a byproduct of your effort and energy. The best firewood is pointless without someone who knows how to make fire.

And then, once the kindling has caught and more has been added, when the fire is raging, when it crackles and glows and continues with only the slightest effort, then you can sit back and enjoy the fruits of your work. Look at that. Feel that heat.

That is communication and sales. The result needs its beginning; the beginning is part of it. You have to put in the work to listen, to be present, to care and be useful and worthy of helping others. And then, once you've become what you will become, you can sit back and say, "Look at that. Feel that heat."

· · ·

TASK

Two things –

1

Do this every morning.

Make sure it's quiet (turn off your phone, television, etc.) and that you're alone.

Sit.

Choose a point across the room – something directly in your field of vision – and focus on it for five uninterrupted minutes. Try to give this spot all your attention, the full weight of your serenity. Don't stand, don't check your phone, don't try to make it 'entertaining.' Just be in the space with yourself and the object of your focus.

This is exceptionally good practice for effective communication. Active attention, patience and the surrender of distractions send a signal that you're physically and emotionally present.

2

Practice listening!

I'm amazed how often the people who most want input, dialogue and feedback don't give other people in the room time to talk. Talking is a dance, and you must assure the other that you are an expert partner. This pact is ruined by interruptions and unsteady attention.

So, make a conscious effort to listen. Make a conscious effort not to interrupt. Make a conscious effort not to impose your point of view on everything.

I think you'll be surprised how difficult this is initially.

And after, I know you'll be surprised what you learn and how much you gain.

"*Where there is the necessary technical skill to move mountains
there is no need for faith that moves mountains.*"

– Eric Hoffer

"*The best way to find yourself is to
lose yourself in the service of others.*"

– Mahatma Gandhi

CHAPTER 7
A.I.D.A.R.S.

How do we make decisions?

Good selling is about helping someone make a positive choice, and good buying is about making positive choices. What, then, is a choice? Why do we make some and forego or forestall others? What are decisions really about?

Zig Ziglar said that in any sale there are five basic obstacles:

- *No need*
- *No money*
- *No hurry*
- *No desire*
- *No trust*

We see this reflected in our own decision-making processes, don't we? What questions do we ask before deciding to do anything? We ask – and must answer Yes to – some combination of those same obstacles:

- Do I **need** it?
- Can I **afford** it?
- Do I need it **now**?
- Do I **want** it?
- Do I **trust** I'll get it?

The Top Performer acknowledges the importance of each question and concern, and does everything in their power to address each, first in the quality of their product or offering, then in the quality of themselves as that product's representative.

. . .

AIDARS.

A word that has served me well for over four decades of sales and coaching. AIDARS is an acronym that will remind you of the six steps to professional selling.

Commit each step to memory. Continually review them in your mind and actions, until it becomes a habit to consciously incorporate each step into every meeting and sales presentation.

The six AIDARS steps are –

- A Attention
- I Interest
- D Desire
- A Action
- R Results
- S Service

The basic methodology behind each step is as follows (we will go into greater detail shortly) –

Attention

You must get the prospect's attention. This involves the activity of the conscious mind.

Interest

You must coax the prospect's interest in your idea. This involves the activity of the conscious mind, and leads to the harmonious activity of the subconscious/emotional mind.

Desire

The prospect should want what you have. This involves the activity of the subconscious mind and leads to physical activity.

Action

Take action. Ask for what you want. (If you can't close, you can't sell.) You must give the prospect a directive to agree to. This involves the physical expression of mental activity and indicates the successful completion of Steps 1-4.

Results

You must let your prospect(s) know they're now your client, and your professional responsibility is to be of positive use to them.

Service

You must work to maintain this professional relationship. Proper service ensures your client doesn't become someone else's prospect. This involves long-term excellence and professional service, which always leads to additional sales and a never-ending flow of new prospects.

• • •

Top Performers understand that in the mind of every prospect there are always two questions:

Can this person be sensitive to me? Can I have confidence in this person?

In other words:

Do you understand me? Can you help me?

We all want to be heard, understood and helped. Every one of us. To that end, as you go through the AIDARS steps, it's important to measure whether or not you're answering those most fundamental human questions. Your ability to provide high quality answers will determine the scope of your success.

• • •

Let's take a closer look at each of the AIDARS steps.

ATTENTION

When you first meet a prospect, *their mind isn't on you.* If you believe you should automatically be given true attention – if you think you're *owed* that – forget it. You must earn the right to sell.

The Top Performer's first objective, then, is to persuade the prospect to stop thinking about whatever they're thinking about, and start thinking about your product or service. Becoming an expert at breaking the preoccupation barrier will make an immeasurable difference in your performance.

The Law of Vibration is worth repeating here as it's essential to the fluid functioning of AIDARS: All things vibrate. From the electron to the universe, everything's constantly in motion. Nothing rests.

To wit, our brains are comprised of billions of cells which are in a constant state of vibration. Whenever an image is presented to your senses, it's implanted in your braincells.

Needless to say, your prospect has an enormous number of images locked away in his or her brain. When a message (sight, sound, touch, smell, taste) is in harmonious vibration with a particular group of brain cells, those cells increase in amplitude of vibration, and the image that's been implanted in those cells flashes on the screen of their mind. This is why certain sounds, sights, smells, etc., can trigger very specific memories without any conscious effort.

And so, in a sales meeting, the Top Performer's objective is to activate the cells that contain and conjure the picture *you want the prospect to think about and concentrate on.* You'll get a prospect's attention by making them aware that you could improve their quality of life and helping them picture that life. The image is going to remain on the screen of their mind as long as the cells holding that image are kept in an increased rate of vibration. This will require you to stay focused on the positive, focused on the good, and embody it with your words, actions and presence.

Now, as you transmit those images and vibrations, you're creating a connection between the prospect's consciousness and yours.

If you aren't paying attention, they won't pay attention either.

The Top Performer's first prerequisite is focused personal attention, which becomes shared, collaborative attention.

INTEREST

This takes us right back to asking questions and listening intently.

If you want interest from your prospect you must be interested yourself. Top Performers are totally involved, mentally and emotionally, in the task at hand. This can't be faked. You must be sincerely interested in helping the prospect improve the quality of their life.

For unlike the conscious mind, the subconscious mind never lies. It's the feeling, unthinking, purely reactive part of your personality. True to the Law of Vibration, you'll always telegraph the images you're emotionally invested in. Whatever strong feelings are being transmitted by the salesperson, those same feelings will populate the harmonic field around them, and the tone projected by them.

Top Performers don't just *act* generous, they *are* generous.

And generosity and enthusiasm, when attached to a valuable product, produces interest.

Once you have the prospect's attention, start asking *questions*. A skillful questioning process will help you determine the key issues in the prospect's mind, and by concentrating on those issues you'll get interested in them yourself. Create in the prospect's mind a healthy dissatisfaction with the status quo.

It's important that your questions be open ended. Rudyard Kipling wrote –

I keep six honest serving men

(they taught me all I knew)

Their names are What and

Why and When

And How and Where and Who.

Open ended questions are powerful. They circulate energy and ideas; they generate solutions; they make new and better futures out of thin air.

What do you mean by that?

Why do you think haven't you done that yet?

When do you expect to know?

How do you plan to accomplish that?

Where do you hope to be a year from now?

Who are you most inspired and influenced by in your work?

By asking the right questions you're going to direct your prospect on the path to providing their own solutions to their needs, wants and objectives. People will never believe something until they discover it for themselves. We become most excited and empowered when we feel like we're solving our own problems.

Ask, actively listen, compassionately respond and you'll encourage the prospect to buy – happily, enthusiastically – without being sold.

Desire

Wallace D. wattles famously said –

"Desire is the effort of the unexpressed possibility within, seeking expression without."

There are only two reasons why anyone will buy anything: to gain a profit or avoid a loss.

Once your prospect can see how their life might improve (i.e. gain or avoid loss) through working with you, they'll want to give that vision material expression. This is desire, and it gains strength the more it's imagined, encouraged and dwelt upon. Excitement is good. Imagination is good. When we say the prospect will develop greater interest, all we mean is they're giving more energy to a new and fabulous idea.

This is when your prospect starts to want what you, the Top Performer has to offer. We've planted the idea in their mind; we've gotten attention, asked questions, listened intently, found their interest, combined it with your product and given that idea back to them. Thinking and speaking have become emotional investment and emotional energy.

This is when the two of you are working as one personality for the good of the prospect. A composite has been formed when your conscious mind clicks into harmony with theirs, and their body moves into action saying,*"I'll improve the quality of my life by using your product/service."*

By becoming invested with you, the prospect is saying I trust you. I have faith in you. Top Performers value that exchange and never betray that trust.

Action

I believe the idea of 'closing' a sale, though crucial, has become over-emphasized. It's merely the natural conclusion to an orderly presentation and fulfilling interaction. You have shown your prospect a way to a better life. To fulfill your vision for a better life, you must formulate a plan of action. The 'close' becomes the action that should reasonably follow.

The prospect is now relying on you and trusting in you for advice, for a way forward from this place of undirected desire. You're now in a position to make a suggestion. Let's think about suggestion for a moment –

It's a term that's used to describe the entrance of ideas into the mind, ideas that are intended to change the existing mental state of a person or group of people. Many treat the idea of suggestion as a trick or cheap manipulation. Not the Top Performer. Suggestion arising from knowledge and experience is one of the most valuable tools the Top Performer has. Suggestion naturally flows from grasping a problem and knowing a solution.

Self-confidence is absolutely necessary to the practice of suggestion. (Remember: *confidence is strength with style*). The more faith a Top Performer has in their power to lead others with true and proper suggestion, the greater their success in the sales arena will be.

If you don't act – if you don't say, *I can help and here's how!* – you won't inspire action in others. There are hundreds of time-tested methods for closing a sale but unless you ask for your objective, even the most polished preliminaries won't bring home the bacon.

Speak up. Seize the moment.

RESULTS

Jack Dixon said –

> *If you focus on results you will never change.*
> *If you focus on change you will get results.*

A sale is a decision for change. When you make a sale, your prospect has decided to improve their life. Top Performers take this decision extremely seriously. Even small changes can require courage. When closing a sale, immediately inform the prospect that in your mind they've just graduated from being a prospective client of yours to becoming an *actual* client. Let them know this means change for you too. It's now become your professional responsibility to serve them. You are there now to answer questions, to clarify, to guide, to follow-up, to follow-through and to help. In a short amount of time, you must assure them they've done the right thing. Top Performers inoculate their clients, as much as they can, against negatives.

Be willing to back up your talk.

They've made a commitment, and so have you.

SERVICE

Remember –

> "*Whatsoever a man soweth, that shall he also reap.*"

> – Galatians 6:7

Or as Ralph Waldo Emerson put it, the Law of Cause and Effect is "the law of laws." You need not be religious to believe in and live by this most basic of rules.

Top Performers know that they get out of life exactly what they give. You must give to your relationships what you want out of them. As this relates to professional relationships with clients, the Top Performer is always asking –

How can I be of greater service?

Am I properly serving my clients' needs?

Am I keeping in contact, am I following up?

Do my clients know they're appreciated?

If you're doing your job properly, you'll find a steady increase in your referrals. Referrals are an excellent measure of performance.

What's your reputation?

Do your clients recommend you and your services to others?

As your AIDARS skills improve, you'll find that service, more than anything else, leads to additional sales and a never-ending flow of prospects, prosperity, new challenges, and fulfillment.

. . .

We have now concluded the six AIDARS steps.

When you start, they may be difficult to hold in your mind and walk through one-by-one. Give it time. They'll become as natural as conversation itself. Let the process do its own work on you.

If you are genuinely seeking to make a prospect's life a better place than it was when you arrived, you're half way to making the sale.

If you think you can fake this, let me tell you now: **you can't.**

The work that you can do is not to invent slicker phrases or smoother deceptions. The Purpose that reads *me me me me me me me!!!*…is no good. It's not inspiring. It repels enrollment in you. The Top Performer's endeavor is to develop the capacity for caring and attention. If you can convey that, it will win out.

And if you *can't* care that much, *you're in the wrong line of work!*

Review your purpose, visions, and goals. Revise them. Find your calling.

You want to inspire people.

And likewise, this is what the Top Performer should demand from *their* personal and professional life.

Are you being understood and listened to?

Are you getting value from your relationships, services and material goods?

Do you feel proud and enthusiastic about the people you know, the ways you spend time, the things you buy?

Are you loving and being loved in return?

Are you serving and being served in return?

Are you receiving mutual effort and care?

Don't go through your life like a bad salesperson or unsatisfied client.

Don't fake your life.

Live your life!

You are here and time is passing. As the saying goes –

Buy the ticket, take the ride.

. . .

TASK

This is more of a reminder. It might appear this and the previous chapter are encouraging a strictly transactional, opportunistic view of personal relationships. That read would be slightly misguided. AIDARS and effective communications are about deliberately, reliably bringing your highest Self into all interactions (including sales, a forum that can sometimes seem allergic to such energies).

I have long said the key to asking for what you want is enthusiasm without desperation. Enthusiasm is a state of grace, and in order to find it, you must be enthusiastic about your life outside of sales and overtly transactional encounters. So, this is a reminder, as you pursue your professional goals, spend time with the people and things that bring you the most enjoyment.

Once a week (at least once) remember to ask yourself –

Was I happy this week?

Did I have enough fun?

Am I happy with how I chose to spend my time?

Happiness is not something you're given only after getting what you want. Happiness is in the getting of it. Happiness is not something you get from prospects, it's something you share with them.

"*Fear knocked at the door. Faith answered.*
And lo, no one was there."

– Proverb.

"*Decide what you want, decide what you are willing to*
exchange for it. Establish your priorities and go to work."

– H.L. Hunt

CHAPTER 8

MASTERMIND

You have your sights set.

You have your goals, your visions, perhaps even your purpose.

Maybe you're already seeing changes in your life.

Maybe you've already begun to feel like a Top Performer.

But there's still an important piece missing…

You need people to share this journey with. People who inspire and incite you. People who see you as you desire and need to be seen to accomplish this tremendous work. A council, there to vocally and symbolically assure you –

Yes, friend. You have all you need. You're ready to ride out. You're ready to ride out with the best of them.

You need other Top Performers.

What you consistently see is what you will consistently be. The forum through which like-minded people share these principles and get together to hold each other accountable to their dreams, we call the Mastermind.

• • •

WHAT IS THE MASTERMIND?

"The Mastermind is an alliance of two or more people working in harmony with positive mental attitude toward a definite end."

– Napoleon Hill

A Mastermind is your own private think tank, your consulting group, your team.

Its members can have pursuits and interests of all kinds, but they share a belief. They believe that the Mastermind group, which is to say what's generated when the group comes together – the energy and intelligence of that collective vibration – creates something greater than any individual is capable of creating on their own.

To this group you'll bring regular updates on your goals, visions and purpose, but also your challenges, your strategic blocks and your frustrations that require feedback to work through. And you'll bring yourself as a trust-worthy, emphatic resource to the other members of the Mastermind group.

You will **never** bring negativity, whining and aimless complaints. Mastermind groups are a place where work is done and progress is made. Their purpose is upward movement. Shared ascent is what happens in a Mastermind group. This is the intention; this is the tone; nothing else.

That explicit, non-negotiable intentionality is where the Mastermind truly distinguishes itself. You might be thinking, *If I'm stuck, frustrated or sad pursuing a goal, why don't I just call my friend? Why do I need a Mastermind group?* The answer – Because your friend is not necessarily committed on that specific day, at that specific time, to bringing what you need to push past your frustrations.

Friendships can be about many things at any given moment. *Mastermind groups are about success and winning at the terms you've set regarding what's required to live your best life.*

So, it's important you don't use other groups or gatherings as substitutes for a Mastermind.

A book club is not a Mastermind group.

A meditation class is not a Mastermind group.

A fantasy football league is not a Mastermind group.

Therapy is not a Mastermind group.

These are all lovely and valuable things to have in one's life. For some, they're indispensable. But just as those spaces can be made sacred, the Master-mind Group is also a sacred space. It's a workshop, yes, but a workshop with particular commitments and particular foundational beliefs and practices.

It's a council that holds you accountable to your own best imagination.

...

MASTERMIND GROUP GUIDELINES.

Most of all, you need a group of people capable of seeing you as your higher self. In other words, what you *envision yourself* to be, and not necessarily the person you show up as on a day-to-day basis. This commitment to aspirational sight – to seeing people as their possibility – is crucial and profound. Not everyone can do it, and not everyone can maintain it.

This orientation is closely tied to the questions that are asked in each Mastermind meeting. Mary Morrissey is fond of saying –

The quality of questions we ask determine the quality of life we lead.

Simple, but so true.

For example, let's say the question you're asking is *Why can't I get a raise?*

What's going to show up, then, is *all the reasons why you can't get the raise.* And once your mind starts searching for those answers, it lowers your entire vibration. What a terrible, low-quality question! What a low vibrational question! It does you absolutely no good!

The better questions, of course, are *How can I be the best at my job? How can I make sure my value is reflected in my pay? How can I do great work and become rich?* These questions raise your vibration, and expectations, do they not?

One of the main tasks of the Mastermind is an insistence on high quality questions. And you, as a group member, bring that elevation both to what you ask and what you give. As a Top Performer, associate yourself with people who will demand high quality questions and answers of you.

A note on the composition of your Mastermind group –

You don't have to find people who are consciously pursuing 'new thought' or 'self-improvement' per se. However, I recommend you keep in mind that it's a skill to see people as their possibilities, to hold them that way and hold them accountable that way. Without some background and some of this work, it can be difficult to find this quality in an assembly of people. The fact is, what's more common in our culture is agreement about limitation. What people tend to do – even in a Mastermind – is to believe in and argue for their limitations. You need people in a Mastermind who can hear that and self-correct, instead of getting sucked into negativity.

If you're not vigilant, what happens more often than not (if you don't have a skillful Mastermind group) is people coming to agreement about the limitations instead of the possibilities. So be advised: choose your group carefully.

A Mastermind group is an active agreement about infinite possibility, and Top Performers are all about possibility. Top Performers live in possibility!

. . .

TEN STEPS TO THE MASTERMIND MEETING

The Mastermind meeting can be broken down to the following 10 steps and guidelines. These are not rigid rules, to be followed letter-perfectly. You have room for customization and improvisation within this structure. *However, the structure is important!* A Mastermind meeting is not a hang-out or a make-your-own salad. Like any sport or club, it possesses distinguishing features and requirements that make it unique. I recommend making alterations only by unanimous vote, and only on a temporary or trial basis.

1

A Mastermind group works best with 2-10 members and no more than 12. There'll be time constraints with more than a dozen members, and the problem of a narrow spectrum of experience with three or less. In my experience, around five to eight members is ideal.

2

Meet regularly. Weekly is suggested. Have a pre-planned agenda to follow. It's best to have a Leader, Time Keeper, and Note Taker assigned ahead of time (with all members rotating these roles).

3

If the Mastermind members are in different cities, the meeting can be conducted via conference call, video conference or any other format that facilitates the most effective communication.

4

Ensure the call is timely and efficient. If you've committed to a one hour call, keep it within that time frame. No more, no less. Time is important; spend it wisely. The Leader should keep the meeting running smoothly, with the Time Keeper responsible for timing each person's participation to see that everything is kept on track. Additionally, the Note Taker's role is critical for any necessary or requested recap and review.

5
Roll Call.

The group Leader should welcome each member as they join the meeting, and assign each person a number (if there are five people in the meeting, the numbers will be one through five). This numbering system is used to designate the order in which each Mastermind member will speak.

6

Begin meetings by reading aloud the seven Mastermind Principles, followed by the Dedication and Covenant. The seven Principles can all be read by the meeting Leader, or you may choose to have a different person read each Principle. The Dedication and Covenant can also be read by one person, though I prefer to have the entire group say it aloud together.

7 Mastermind Principles

I RELEASE myself to the Mastermind because I am strong when I have others to help me.

I BELIEVE the combined intelligence of the Mastermind creates a wisdom far beyond my own.

I UNDERSTAND that I will more easily create positive results in my life when I am open to looking at myself, my problems and my opportunities from another's point of view

I DECIDE to release my desire totally in trust to the Mastermind and I am open to accepting new possibilities.

I FORGIVE myself for mistakes I have made. I also forgive others who have hurt me in the past so I can move into the future with a clean slate.

I ASK the Mastermind to hear what I really want; and I hear my Mastermind partners supporting me in my fulfillment.

I ACCEPT, I know and I relax, believing that the working power of the Mastermind will respond to my every need. I am grateful knowing this is so.

Dedication & Covenant
(if you prefer to keep your Mastermind meeting secular,
ignore the portions in brackets [ ])

I now have a covenant in which it is agreed that the Mastermind shall supply me with an abundance of all things necessary to live a success-filled and happy life.

I dedicate myself to be of maximum service to [God and] my fellow human beings, to live in a manner that will set the highest example for others to follow and to remain an open channel [for God's will].

I go forth with a spirit of enthusiasm, excitement and expectancy.

7
Good News –

Start the sharing portion of the meeting with each Mastermind member sharing their 'win' for the week. Say something good that happened, that you took part in. What's your best work since the last meeting? What's your best moment? This gets the meeting started in a positive vibration. Allow each person one to two minutes to share their win.

8
Feedback & Support –

To ensure maximum benefit to everyone, each Mastermind member needs to be prepared for the meeting. The Time Keeper determines how much time each person is allocated, making certain to leave a little time at the meeting's end for agreeing who will lead, time keep, and take notes on the next meeting.

It's important that everyone understands the amount of time allotted is both to state their request and receive the group's response. (for example, if the total time allocated for each member is four minutes, and it takes three minutes for that member to state their request for feedback and support, it allows the group only a minute to respond.)

At the end of each member's time, the time keeper will gently say something to the effect of "Time is up," and the next person will begin.

This structure is one of the important pillars of a Mastermind meeting. One of the easiest ways to keep the integrity of the meeting – because it's very easy for a meeting to degenerate into time-consuming chit chat – is structure.

A fantastic thing about time constraints is they force you to hone in on problems that have been nebulous in your head. You build the skill of speaking what you're after, then how to pose that objective as a quality question. And the more you pose quality questions to the Mastermind group, the more you internalize quality questions yourself.

9

Each Mastermind group member should be supported – emotionally, verbally and practically – by the other members. For example: Someone wants a new home. One member might say, "I see you driving up to your glorious new home, and I see your children running through your grassy yard." Or another member might provide contact information for a resource in real estate. The principle is that we believe for others what they cannot fully believe for themselves. These are not idle words. You must create and project to the Mastermind a clear vision of what the words represent.

10

Depending on the length of your meeting and the number in attendance, you may decide to leave room for unstructured, open discussion at the end, at which time everyone will have a chance to speak.

• • •

To start, try being in a Mastermind group for six months. Give it your best. Measure your results as you go. I believe you'll see a robust improvement in your results.

Participating in a Mastermind is a way of life that elevates your game. Your life starts to show up differently. If you understand the Laws of Attraction and Vibration – that like attracts like – you want to be around people who will model the qualities you want to embody.

The Mastermind gets you vibrating at the level of the things you desire, creating incredible momentum in the direction your intentions are set.

Try it. You'll see.

• • •

TASK

You probably saw this one coming –

Start or join a Mastermind group.

If you know people whose aspirations, accomplishments and vibration level you admire who have already formed a Mastermind group, ask to join.

If you want to start a Mastermind group yourself, make a list of people you think are a good fit, and start asking. Remember, you don't have to share the same ambitions, style or even location. Variety is good. Diversity of experience and opinion is good.

The important thing is to share a belief and commitment to the structure(s) detailed in the Chapter. Trust and reliability are critical. Choose people you admire. Choose people who you see, and who see you. Choose a team you'll be proud to be part of.

"I can't change the direction of the wind,
But I can adjust my sails to always reach my destination."

– Jimmy Dean

"Step out of the history that is holding you back.
Step into the new story you are willing to create."

– Oprah Winfrey

CHAPTER 9

TESTIMONIES

I've given you a lot to think about and work with. In this chapter, I'm sharing some testimonies of how people have used this advice to make significant, positive changes in their lives and the lives of those around them.

...

ANGIE TAN

I first met John Kanary in 2006, while attending a seminar he and his business partner were doing with Great Eastern Life in Singapore. I found the Top Performer concepts incredibly compelling and subsequently signed up with John as a personal coach/mentor.

At that time, I was doing well in my business career. My production each year was about $80K, with an annual income of about $250K to $300K as a producer; I was hitting benchmarks at a high rate and had begun to serve in management capacities, recruiting and overseeing new agents. It was easy to motivate myself, but I wasn't confident motivating others. How do you help someone else set high goals and achieve their potential? How do you teach and transfer the things you're 'doing right'? How do you identify what you're doing right in the first place?!

But after some time working with John and the Top Performer concepts, I realized there was a whole curriculum of things that I was 'doing right.' My success wasn't random. I had a system, and that system could be learned.

I'd been a teacher prior to joining the insurance industry. As both a teacher and salesperson, I was systematic and disciplined in planning my schedule and making records of all my activities on a daily basis. I kept lists, reviewed them every night, measured my progress, designed new plans and set new goals.

Throughout the years, I had executed this routine under the assumption it was purely administrative, never taking stock of the impact it had on my *mind*. Never noticing that I had made a habit, every day, of visualizing myself reaching my goals and imagining how to best serve my clients. I was creating my life by accident…but also on purpose!

Once I had this revelation, I began to spend more time on such activities, no longer seeing them as administrative duties, but rather exercises to strengthen and expand my mind and heart.

I continued to use the system of recording my activities and updating my progress each day. However, following Top Performer principles, I paid more attention to my *thinking*. I hold only positive thoughts in my mind while evaluating my goals. This leads to a positive feeling, thus creating a positive action, which then brings about positive (desired) results.

Whenever a negative thought comes to mind, if it's a real objection or obstacle, I ask myself how I can *counter* that obstacle. Who and where are the resources that I can call on to overcome this? Even if the problem or issue may not seem to have a solution, I tell myself that **the solution is out there**. *Something can be done.* With this, I continue to persist to search for the solution (or the how) until the 'miracle' happens. If a goal is worth achieving, I break it down into smaller milestones and simply work on the activities every day.

I also learned through John and Top Performer to let my subconscious mind 'go to work'. The subconscious mind is an incredible problem solver. When given a problem, I often make an effort to think of it – calmly, with interest but without anxiety – right before bed. I've been able to solve many problems big and small with this method. Your mind can be like a team of Santa's elves – it has a bundle of presents ready for you by morning.

Over the years working with Top Performer, my confidence and results have improved exponentially. I now run a team of 20 people. We consistently meet and exceed our company's highest benchmarks of production on individual and team levels. My income and leisure time have more than tripled. I work hard and play hard. I am able to travel about three months a year, to conventions, vacations and missions with my church, all of which feeds and enriches my spirit and the work I do. In short, as John is fond of saying –

Life is 'wunderful!' (with the *U* in it, because *U* made it so!)

. . .

RICK SPENCE

A brief story of the Three Amigos.

There's a famous proverb:

If you want to go fast, go alone. If you want to go far, go together.

I believe there are two roads you can travel in life. The first road is easy, quicker, less bumpy, but not often to the benefit of all involved. It's a shortcut and it comes with a price. Every shortcut costs something.

The second road is more difficult – full of twists and turns, and much longer. It's far more challenging, but more rewarding, and truly for the best interest of everyone on the journey.

Today I run a financial planning practice that manages approximately 120 million on behalf of 500 families.

But years ago, I was walking the first road. I was going fast, and I was going alone. (Of course, I didn't know it at the time – one of the most appealing qualities of the first road is ignorance. You only learn you're on it after you've left.)

Then I met John Kanary, and began working according to the ideas of Top Performer.

When you have a mentor, this individual makes it their personal mission to help you be a better person. John, with his infinite wisdom, recognized that three of his students/friends – myself and two other guys, all working at the same company – had shared interests, dreams, and ideas about how business could be done. He suspected we'd receive greater rewards from his mentorship as a group than individually.

We began collaborating, working as a team, coaching each other and brainstorming together. We came to be known at The Three Amigos.

The Three Amigos represent the second road. We place everyone's best interests before our own. We dedicate ourselves to improving the lives of our family, friends, work associates, and everyone we come in contact with. By persistently working together to be the best version of ourselves we can be, we have all, despite many challenges, improved our personal and professional lives in ways we never could have planned. It's a dream, and it's better than dreaming.

The second road comes with a cost too.

We've sometimes had to pass on opportunities in order to protect the balance and atmosphere we've so worked hard to achieve. But that's part of reaching your visions – learning it's okay to say no. No can be a beautiful, empowering word.

Like the tortoise racing the hare, the Three Amigos might appear slow, but through steadfast friendship and careful planning, we travel far and are victorious in the end.

. . .

SANDY KENNEDY

I met John Kanary in Toronto, 1988. He was hosting a seminar called Born Rich with Bob Proctor – his partner at the time. I had just gotten my real estate license. I have an undergraduate degree in engineering and an MBA in business administration and marketing. I had left my job with a large telecommunications company to pursue commission sales in Real Estate.

I was born in Charlottetown, Prince Edward Island – the smallest province in Canada – and lived there until I was 19. The main Prince Edward Island industries are farming, fishing and tourism. Being a successful businessman is not something you typically aspire to growing up in those communities.

At that time, to be honest, I was a 'blank piece of paper.' I was 28 years old, living in Toronto and in my heart, I *knew* I wasn't happy. I was working as an engineering manager, and I can remember looking at my boss and thinking, *I don't want your job! You make 10k a year more than me but you have 10 times the stress. I don't want any of this.*

There was, quite simply, no motivation to stay. If I didn't want my boss' job, or my boss' boss' job, what was I doing? Just putting in time? Just wasting time?

I was single with no dependents, and I thought, *If I hurt anybody, it will only be me. My heart tells me there's something else out there.*

I had always had some interest in real estate. I bought my first home as soon as I graduated, and it had gone up in value dramatically in the few years I worked at the telecommunications company. I liked talking, reading and thinking about real estate.It seemed a natural fit.

So I entered the seminar with an open mind, which John and Bob filled with positive thoughts. I certainly didn't imagine having the success I've had, but *Born Rich* and John's *Top Performer* principles immediately and dramatically raised my expectations as to what is and isn't reasonable and possible.

The premise of Top Performer was compelling and clear – *You can do whatever you want. There's no limit. There's no ceiling.* That was the claim.

So naturally, I looked at this premise and thought, *If this is true.... tell me more. Prove it. Show me. I'm a scientist by training, so show me. Give me evidence.*

A vision had begun to take shape in my mind: I wanted to be the top real estate agent in Canada.

In my case, it wasn't hard to find evidence that it was possible, because there were other people around me who had already done it. John gave me a simple directive.

Find the previous top real estate agents in Canada.

Meet them.

Interview them.

See what they're like, how they live. Find out what your vision is made of. Find out what it actually takes.

Okay…

That process became a huge eye opener. I came to see – they had no skills that I didn't. If they could make what they were making with their abilities, I'd have no problem at all. I could do that and more.

And the sky was the limit at that point.

I knew there were changes coming and that some might be painful, but that my current life didn't fit the new me.

The lesson I had to learn was that if you keep doing what you've always been doing, you're going to get the same results. If you want to make big changes in your life, you have to be prepared to make big changes in your attitudes and actions.

The changes were almost immediate. My outcomes grew and grew. My circle of friends and colleagues expanded. I met my wife of 27 years and counting.

Being a Top Performer is, of course, an ongoing process. There's no one answer.

You read books or come out of seminars on an incredible emotional high. Then you have to deal with the realities of life, the setbacks of life, as there always are, (including for me).

But the important thing about internalizing Top Performer methods is to go forward with the knowledge that *Yes, this can be done.* When you have the down times, you have to be able to lift yourself up quickly, and that means surrounding yourself with good people who are positive and like-minded.

For me that meant forming a Mastermind group. I formed one in 1989 with a few close colleagues, and it still exists to this day. The group has gone from being Toronto local to Canada-wide, with a network of over 100 members.

Because we all have bad days. We all have negative thoughts. We all lose our inspiration sometimes. But you have to take those setbacks as coaching experiences along the way.

The good producers, the Top Performers, get back up quicker. They go down into valleys, but don't stay long. Live your setbacks, breathe them, then learn what you have to learn and move on to the next step, whatever that may be.

By 2001, I was the top real estate agent in Canada, and I remain in the top tier of my profession to this day.

I'm still growing, still accomplishing, still looking for the next vision that will challenge my ideas of what's possible.

. . .

Aaron Tan

To future Top Performers –

On this topic, I owe so much to my mentor, Mr. John Kanary, for teaching me new paradigms, expanding my horizons and for believing in me through all the ups and downs.

With each lesson, I've learned that the future Top Performer can be *anyone*. A Top Performer isn't necessarily the wealthiest, most talented, most charismatic person in the room, because those are all relative to each individual. What's important is that you understand you can be a Top Performer, that you can define what it means for yourself, and you believe in your dreams wholeheartedly, with no reservations.

Another great tip I'd like to share is becoming a Top Performer doesn't even need to be in the 'future.' It can happen now, at this moment, in your mind and imagination, the instant you begin to believe. Once that absolute belief takes hold of your subconscious, magical things start to happen.

Time is relative, a concept and unit of measurement conceived by man and if that's the case, all the more we should use 'time' to our advantage.

In this day and age, when almost every bit of information known to man is available to everybody who is literate and has access to the internet, the playing field in terms of knowledge has been leveled at a historically unprecedented scale. The challenge, then, is to determine what knowledge is most useful to you, to absorb it, to surround yourself with positivity. Then it's a matter of feeding your mind *consciously*, almost *obsessively*, with a vision of yourself as the Top Performer you'll become.

Before long, you'll speak, think and feel it into existence.

It's my sincere wish for each and every one of you reading this book, to remember the moment you decided to be a Top Performer, and to inspire others to take the same route. As the saying goes – *there's always room at the top.*

I wish you happiness, health and wealth in your journey ahead.

"One is never afraid of the unknown;
one is afraid of the known coming to an end."

– Jiddu Krishnamurti

"Impossible is just a big word thrown around by small men who
find it easier to live in the world they've been given than to
explore the power they have to change it. Impossible is not a fact.
It's an opinion. Impossible is not a declaration.
It's a dare. Impossible is potential. Impossible is temporary.
Impossible is nothing."

– Muhammad Ali

CHAPTER 10
WHAT NEXT?

Great achievements require great achievers.

You are now well on your way to becoming a Top Performer. You know what you must do, and you know what's coming.

Have you set your First Vision? Have you started to pursue it? What's your first goal? What's your next goal?

Although you've reached the final pages, rest assured this is not the end of this book's usefulness. Keep it close, write in its margins, return to it whenever you need a boost of inspiration, a reminder of the proper function of any Top Performer steps, or a check-in with yourself and your reasons for doing what you do and being who you are.

These words will be here, ready.

I will be here, ready.

Let's review –

...

ATTITUDE AND EXPECTATIONS

First, who are you?

How do you see yourself? Do you believe you're meant for better things? What's the character of your spirit, and is that the vibration you're putting into the world?

Prepare for this journey. Spiritually align yourself with the You you aspire to be, the You you can imagine yourself becoming.

Do you expect happiness?

Do you expect joy?

Do you expect the exceptional?

You have your achievement pyramid. Are you ready to fill it? Are you ready to make it so?

. . .

GOALS

Are you setting A, B, or C Goals?

Are you doing what you've done before, or are you transcending your past and previous paradigms?

Are your goals *strategic*? (are they taking you directly toward your visions?)

Are you accomplishing – or accomplishing pieces of – your goals every day?

Are your goals in harmonic resonance with your visions and purpose?

Where are your goals taking you? Into what bright frontiers? Toward what marvelous vision(s)?

. . .

VISIONS

Are your visions authentic to you? (i.e. have you created them through internal reflection and creative speech?)

Can you picture your vision(s), your future, in macro and micro detail?

How does imagining the vision make you feel?

Does the sum of your visions surpass the mere addition of goals?

Is achieving your goals bringing you closer to your vision(s)?

Are your visions holistic (will reaching them involve excellence in multiple aspects of life?)

Is achieving your vision(s) giving birth to new, ambitious, informed, exciting visions?

. . .

PURPOSE

What is your Big Why?

Does it fill you with inspiration, humility, awe, ambition and delight?

Can you feel it in your bones? Does every cell in your body cry out *"Yes, yes, yes, this is what I'm made to do?"*

Can you say your purpose out loud?

Can you write your purpose clearly?

Does your purpose benefit you and the world? Will living it bring good to others?

Is your purpose an infinite game? (i.e. can it ever be finished? can it ever be mastered?)

Are you playing it?

• • •

EFFECTIVE COMMUNICATION

When necessary, are you able to communicate and exchange information toward a desired result?

Do you share? Do you listen? Are you fully present?

Do you take the time to know people's name(s) and personal details?

Do you expect to achieve the results you want?

Do you have a healthy relationship to criticism? Are you able to use it as intelligent fuel for improvement?

Are you confident? (NOT do you seem confident – are you ACTUALLY confident?)

Are you direct and to-the-point?

Are you sincere and authentic?

Are you friendly and kind?

Do you constantly strive to find the good in failure, disappointment and accident, as well as success?

• • •

AIDARS

How do you show up for both the new and established relationships in your life?

Do you work to understand, to listen, to be understood?

Are you brave enough to be vulnerable in front of other people?

Are you brave enough to be honest in front of other people?

Are you on the same vibration as the people in your life?

Do you ask for what you want?

Are you adding value to the lives of others?

What is your reputation among the people who know you?

Are you being of service?

Do you create and keep high quality relationships?

Do you care? Do you show it? How do you show it?

. . .

MASTERMIND/COACHING

Have you found a Mastermind group?

Do you meet regularly?

Do your Mastermind meetings follow a reliable and effective routine?

Are they holding you accountable to your objectives?

Are you holding them accountable to their objectives?

Are you and your Mastermind group engaged in an agreement of mutual excellence?

Do you see the best in each other and bring it out?

Are you seeing results? Are they the results you want?

. . .

If you're feeling overwhelmed… **don't**

Settle down…

Breathe…

Relax…

I have good news….

As you incorporate the Top Performer principles into your life, you'll discover something fantastic.

Most of these practices overlap and flow into each other. Doing one often leads, through logical and natural progressions, to doing many at once.

For example –

I had a client with a simple goal: he wanted to begin jogging for exercise.

He'd been putting it off for years. "There's no time. I'm too busy," he'd say (sound familiar?). But then he left his job for a better position at another company, and in the pocket of time between jobs, he hadn't even purchased running sneakers.

So, we set an even simpler goal…

Go jogging once.

Just once.

Tomorrow morning. No excuses. No delays. No matter what.

He went running the next morning. He called me after – exhausted, sore, out of breath…and **completely ecstatic**. "I had no idea," he said. "All that time. Why did I wait all that time?.."

He began a steady routine of running (goal), which also caused him to lose weight (goal), which also required him to improve his diet (goal), for which he learned to cook (goal), all of which reduced his stress (goal) and made him a happier person at his new job, with healthier relationships to his new colleagues (vision).

His knees don't have the spring they did when he began, and he has since pivoted to another career path, but he still runs.

Of course, this is a particular case, but you see how accomplishing one objective, with intention and an open heart, can have a branching effect that spreads outward, begetting a wealth of unforeseen improvements in a Top Performer's life.

• • •

Here, once more, let's look at the **10 Characteristics of Top Performers**

I

The Top Performer understands there is no known method by which anyone can determine what you can accomplish in a given period of time. Your potential as a Top Performer is boundless.

II

Top Performers are continually improving their results while decreasing their workload.

III

Top Performers are continually accomplishing more in shorter periods of time.

IV

Top Performers continually have a goal or objective that they're pursuing.

V

Top Performers must be able to see how they can reach their goals by improving their effectiveness in the necessary areas of their lives.

VI

Top Performers are emotionally involved in the achievement of their goals, visions and purpose.

VII

Top Performers continually operate on a creative plain, never on a competitive plain. They never allow standards or precedents to influence their objectives.

VIII

The Top Performer is acutely aware of the difference between work and leisure.

IX

The Top Performer always keeps service and the well-being of others foremost in their mind.

X

The Top Performer is always involved in a planned program of personal happiness and self- development.

. . .

These qualities are the natural result of doing the work outlined in this book's chapters. If you're engaged and committed, being a Top Performer must follow. Being a Top performer is inevitable.

You'll have setbacks. Some things won't turn out as you expect. But remember, if you aren't failing, you aren't trying.

On this journey, some unhappiness is inevitable (that's life, after all!). But excessive unhappiness is a waste of time. Excessive unhappiness is self-indulgent. If you're going to indulge, indulge in joy. Indulge in purpose.

Your life is your own…

Live with passion…

Live with volume…

Succeed and keep going…

Fail and keep going…

Make life your art…

Drink deep…

Be part of the world…

Be part of your moment…

Try…

Create…

Love…

Today...

This minute…

Right now.

Congratulations on taking your first steps toward the life you were born to live. The change has already begun.

It's been more than a pleasure for me to share in this program with you.

Thank you so much for being a part of Top Performer.

– John Kanary

AFTERWORD

"A goal is a dream with a deadline,
but having a deadline is merely the beginning."

– Napoleon Hill

You were created for a purpose, and now that you have finished reading this book, it's time to put what you have learned into action.

Every major success begins with discovering your true life's purpose. Finding your true purpose in life is the crucial first step for success. Successful people know their purpose in life. They know their mission and they're doing everything they can to achieve it. They set up goals and visions that will bring them to their purpose. Successful people are happy, fulfilled, and living life with joy!

This book is dripping with inspiration, advice and most importantly, a plan. It lays out the process of achieving your goals step by step and makes that elusive dream feel easy to accomplish. It provides a thorough, well thought out process for achieving your goal, and is a great read as well!

John Kanary, in this book, teaches the exact blueprint to achieve all the goals and dreams you're most excited about.

As a reminder, here are John's 10 Characteristics of Top Performers:

1. The Top Performer understands there's no known method by which anyone can determine what you can accomplish in a given period of time. Your potential as a Top Performer is boundless.

2. Top Performers are continually improving their results while decreasing their workload.

3. Top Performers are continually accomplishing more in shorter periods of time.

4. Top Performers continually have a goal or objective they're pursuing.

5. Top Performers must be able to see how they can reach their goals by improving their effectiveness in the necessary areas of their lives.

6. Top Performers are emotionally involved in the achievement of their goals, visions and purpose.

7. Top Performers continually operate on a creative plain, never on a competitive plain. They never allow standards or precedents to influence their objectives.

8. The Top Performer is acutely aware of the difference between work and leisure.

9. The Top Performer always keeps service and the well-being of others foremost in their mind.

10. The Top Performer is always involved in a planned program of personal happiness and self-development.

This book is also a workbook and productivity planner and was created for the person who's ready to take their life to the next level through a visually stunning and empowering strategic plan.

The book contains the most effective and and powerful productivity tools and techniques including:

– Achievement pyramid

– The A, B, Cs to goal creating

– Tasks at the end of every chapter

– Difference between Goals, Visions and Purpose

– Planning and priority scheduling

– Examples of all of the above

– Testimonials

John has taught us that *"Goals are the small, tactical steps – the strategies – we take to achieve our visions. Goals are short term, visions long term. Your purpose, if articulated honestly, will rarely (if ever) change."*

John Kanary walks you through the complete experience of what it means to set goals and achieve them, and what it means for your visions and purpose. This is something I've rarely seen in other self-help books.

The tasks that John has created at the end of each chapter are designed to motivate, encourage and ultimately, get you to take action.

There are three primary goal types, described as follows:

1. A-Goals: What you know you can do. A Goals are things you have done before and can reliably do again.

2. B-Goals: What you think you can do. B Goals are aspiration without purpose.

3. C Goals: What you want. C Goals are where goals meet purpose.

Everyone's journey in life is different, but the principles of goal-setting, like the laws of physics, are the same for everyone.

After reading this entire book, it's obvious that *The Top Performer* was developed for the achievers in the world; those who have a burning desire to rise up and make a positive impact. Since you've reached this point in this book, I believe you are one of the TOP PERFORMERS that will achieve greatness, make an impact and ascend personally as well as professionally.

This book has given you the tools you need so you can reach your goals QUICKLY and SIMPLY... just the way busy people desire it to be.

So, now how does it feel to know that dream that you hold in your mind is actually possible?

YOU WERE CREATED FOR MORE!

The Top Performer was created for the person who is ready to take their life to the next level through a visually stunning and empowering strategic planning system.

Author John Kanary has created a goal clarification process that will allow you to choose your own top performing goals and put them on the road to achievement while also living on purpose.

This book has simplified everything in your life and has now made your goals crystal clear while at the same time tying your purpose to goal achievement – so you're now clear on how they relate to one another and why that discovery is critical to your ongoing success.

If you're an entrepreneur or sales professional who's constantly trying to improve on your success, this book is a great resource for you, not just to read once, but to continue to come back to. The exercises will continue to help you clarify and analyze your personal goals, leading you to clarity and simplicity when it comes to your visions and purpose.

The benefits and importance of this book help you:

* Change the way you think about goals and goals-setting

* Encourage you to find a purpose

* Help you simplify methods

* Explain the power of thoughts and beliefs

* Understand that achievements are the direct result of thoughts and beliefs

* Know you're becoming the master of your own thoughts, giving energy with inspiration and intentional application to your selected purpose and growth.

* Show you to visualize the steps and instructions while never giving up

* Make yourself ready and arm yourself against what gets in your way

* Show you how to listen to your intuition and instinct (whispers)

* Put a plan on paper, visualize your way to success

It's important to emphasize that life mastery isn't about having it figured out completely and living a purely perfect and flawless life because honestly, that's not how life is. There are ups and downs; there are good times and bad times, and there are times when you make the craziest of decisions and mistakes even if you have mastered your life.

Mastering your life is about figuring out the right direction to take and paying attention to every important area of your life so that you live a well-rounded life that you actually enjoy. Even when you do falter, you'll know you're doing a good job overall and will move forward gracefully.

You've learned all you need to know to master your life and steer it in the direction you want. While you'll need to put in a lot of work to achieve this, the good news is it's actually doable now, thanks to this book.

Enjoy the journey.

Peggy McColl, *New York Times* Best-Selling Author

ABOUT THE AUTHOR

John Kanary has invested forty-six years in the research, development and teaching of personal effectiveness with people in all walks of life, throughout the world. His laser-like energy shifts your thinking to a new level. It inspires creative thought and empowers you to take consistent action.

...

Printed in Great Britain
by Amazon